SHORT WALKS FROM
—————— PUBS IN ——
Middlesex &
West London

David Hall
and Rosemary Hall

COUNTRYSIDE BOOKS
NEWBURY, BERKSHIRE

First published 1996
© David Hall and Rosemary Hall 1996

COUNTRYSIDE BOOKS
3 Catherine Road
Newbury, Berkshire

ISBN 1 85306 426 2

For our parents and families

Designed by Mon Mohan
Cover illustration by Colin Doggett
Photographs by David Hall
Maps by Rosemary Hall

Produced through MRM Associates Ltd., Reading
Printed by J W Arrowsmith Ltd., Bristol

Contents

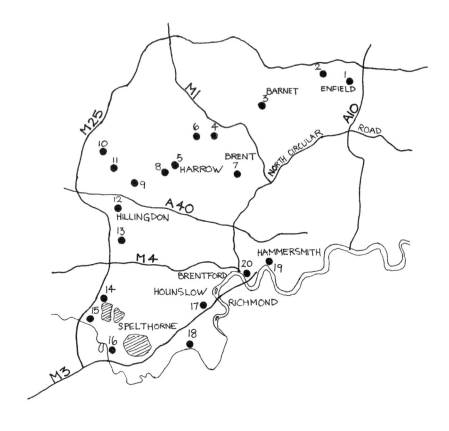

Area map showing the locations of the walks.

Publisher's Note

We hope that you obtain considerable enjoyment from this book; great care has been taken in its preparation. However, changes of landlord and actual closures are sadly not uncommon. Likewise, although at the time of publication all routes followed public rights of way or permitted paths, diversion orders can be made and permissions withdrawn.

We cannot of course be held responsible for such diversion orders and any inaccuracies in the text which result from these or any other changes to the routes nor any damage which might result from walkers trespassing on private property. However, we are anxious that all details covering the walks and the pubs are kept up to date and would therefore welcome information from readers which would be relevant to future editions.

Introduction

Despite recent signs of rethinking on local government boundaries, and the possible re-emergence of Rutland, Middlesex lives on only in the name of sports teams, a station in the Boat Race and as a postal address. Within its old boundaries, however, are some very rewarding walks, and not a few pubs, all easily accessible from the metropolitan area by public transport. We know this, because that's how we went to every single walk. You don't have to drink and drive.

So here are another 20 pleasant strolls with a pub as start and finish point, all within the old county or the adjacent parts of West London, to complement the 30 described in *Pub Walks in Middlesex and West London.* The walks betray our weakness for walking beside water, or better still, between two bodies of water. On a couple of walks, there really is an old mill by the stream – perfect for a walk starting from a pub. Some walks in this highly built-up area are rural, some are along stretches of greenery in the middle of an urban landscape, all offer some opportunity of seeing wildlife. Many walks pass by buildings of historical or architectural interest – one takes you past no less than three museums – and some go through peaceful cemeteries and the last resting places of the rich and famous.

Although the walks are shorter than in the previous book, the research seemed to take longer. Eventually we realised that we were spending longer in the pubs! The standard of pubs seems to have increased appreciably in the last few years, especially as regards food and the comfort in which you can sit and eat it. The 20 pubs we have selected are a diverse bunch, ranging from everyone's ideal local, serving good beer and honest to goodness pub grub, to establishments taking pride in cuisine that surpasses a number of pretentious restaurants, but is much better value for money. Cromwell may have drunk in one, and Charles I certainly visited another; two share the unusual name The Case is Altered. All of them have a friendly atmosphere, and virtually all welcome families. Many are now open all day on Sundays, rather than the traditional Sunday hours of 12 noon to 3 pm and 7 pm to 10.30 pm. We think all of the pubs are worth a visit in their own right.

All of the walks are covered by the OS Landranger map, sheet 176 West London area (1:50,000); for more detail, the relevant 1:25,000 maps are given in each walk. An A–Z or Nicholson street atlas will also be useful for the more central walks. You may find it helpful to carry a compass to follow bearings given to assist you on some walks where there are no obvious landmarks. All of the walks follow public rights of way, permissive paths, or are across public open space, but not all of these are shown on maps. Sometimes this is because the paths are new. Much praise is due to all those responsible for the new Hillingdon Trail, a 20 mile, well-signposted path from Springwell Lock near Rickmansworth south to near Heathrow Airport, parts of which we have incorporated in a couple of walks. In other places, however, the quality of signs and stiles leaves a lot to be desired – perhaps this will improve if the paths are used more often.

Much of the research was carried out in an unprecedented dry period – you may find some walks muddier than we did. Please don't tramp into pubs in muddy boots. If you want to leave a car in the pub car park while you walk, please ask first, even where we've indicated that it's usually alright. Many of the routes are excellent places to exercise dogs, but be prepared to keep dogs outside most pubs, and please don't take dogs into the churchyards and cemeteries on the walks. And remember the motto: take only photographs, leave only footprints.

We wish to thank everyone who helped us along the way, especially David's parents for helping enormously with the initial research, Mrs Sword of Laleham, the voluntary worker at Headstone Manor Tithe Barn, the Herts & Middlesex Wildlife Trust for information about Stocker's Lake, the London Wildlife Trust for information about Crane Park Island, the lost walker in Mad Bess Wood and of course the ever-patient bar staff for answering all our questions.

Enjoy the walks.

David Hall and Rosemary Hall
Spring 1996

Clay Hill
1
The Rose and Crown

The Rose and Crown is a wonderful old inn on the edge of Enfield, dating back to 1712. Inevitably for an ancient hostelry in North London it claims connections with Dick Turpin, highwayman and, obviously, undercover researcher for Ye Goode Beer Guide. Inside, plenty of wooden beams impart a historic atmosphere. The spacious, rambling layout provides a comfortable bar on the left, a seating area near the foot of the central staircase and a bar going through to the back on the right; leather Chesterfields and settles are dotted about. The staircase leads to a first-floor dining area used in busy periods. There is a large outdoor area with benches and tables; the Turkey brook runs alongside the car park.

Food is served from a counter at the back of the right-hand bar from 12 noon to 9 pm (5 pm on Sunday). As well as a number of hot and cold dishes on a constant menu, there are tasty daily specials such as broccoli and cheese bake, spicy meatballs and quiche, all at very reasonable prices and well-presented with salad garnish. Snacks and a range of cold dishes are available. On Sunday, a roast lunch and the usual menu are provided. In the summer, barbecues are held after 5 pm on Saturday and on one or two other evenings every week, depending on the weather ('We refuse to do it in the rain!'). Children are welcome in the upstairs dining area, when this is open, and in the garden.

Drinking hours are: Monday to Saturday 11 am to 11 pm; and Sunday 12 noon to 10.30 pm. The beers served were Theakston Special Bitter, Webster's Yorkshire Bitter and Courage Directors at the time of researching (but this is now a Scottish and Newcastle house).
Telephone: 0181 363 2010.

How to get there: The pub is on Clay Hill, EN2, opposite Hilly Fields Park near Browning Road. From the south, take the A10, go left onto Carterhatch Lane, and continue straight over Baker Street/Forty Hill into Clay Hill. Nearest station: Gordon Hill (BR from Moorgate) is very near the cemetery visited on the walk.

Parking: In the pub car park.

Length of the walk: 3¼ miles. Map: OS Pathfinder 1140 (inn GR 326987).

This is a rural walk which takes you through Hilly Fields Park, with its large variety of fine trees, the adjoining cemetery, which contains a number of imposing Victorian memorials to worthy citizens of Enfield, and the well-wooded Whitewebbs Park which, along with Trent Park, is one of the few surviving remnants of Enfield Chase.

The Walk
From the pub cross Clay Hill and enter Hilly Fields Park at the corner with Browning Road. Take the tarmac path straight ahead through the park, which has lime and oak avenues and silver birches. At the fork bear right, then go straight ahead at the crossroads. Just before the path exits onto Phipps Hatch Lane, stay in the park by turning right onto the path running by a line of oaks. After the second oak tree turn left onto a dirt path. Pass another line of oaks by a picnic bench, then turn immediately left and exit the park onto Cook's Hole Road. Turn left and at the T-junction turn right onto Phipps Hatch Lane. Continue ahead when Phipps Hatch Lane becomes Cedar Road, and enter Lavender Hill Cemetery by the main gate. It is open until 7 pm in summer, 5 pm otherwise.
    Immediately to the right is the impressive tomb of Blanche and James William Moseley. Go left towards the left-hand chapel, passing a number of Gibbons family tombs, and follow the path to the left of the chapel and on round to a tomb marked by a red granite pillar topped by an urn, the Buszard family vault, on an island in the middle of a crossroads. Pass this on your left and continue on, crossing straight over the main drive to go between plots A and D. At the Bosanquet family tomb turn right to approach the second chapel, turn left onto the path beyond it and pass the

9

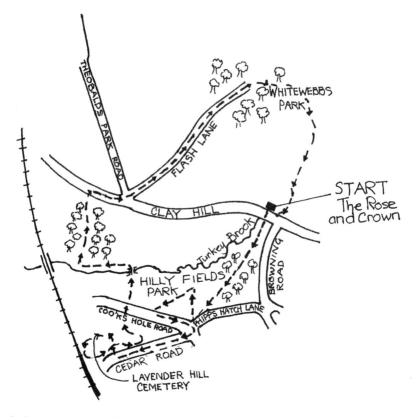

dark Germanic tomb of Heinrich Faulenbach (1854–1904) on the left. At the bench turn left and walk across the grass, passing (on the right) the Lucena family vault surmounted by a charming monument of a child and dog. Continue ahead to pass the Short family vault, marked by a column on an island, take the tarmac path opposite, and then turn right onto a narrower tarmac path. Follow it to the end, and leave the cemetery.

Cross over Cook's Hole Road and re-enter Hilly Fields Park. Walk downhill across the grass to the tarmac path and turn left to walk by the Turkey brook. Turn right at a T-junction just before the thatched cottage ahead on the left, cross the bridge and turn immediately left onto a narrow path threading through trees, following the line of the brook on the left, with a sports field to the right. Cross a ditch, then just as a viaduct comes into view, before a fenced-off area, turn right onto a path heading roughly north. Keep ahead past the trees, following the path as it veers to the right, and then left at the hedge round the sports field and fork right to exit on Strayfield Road.

Lavender Hill cemetery.

Turn right and come to Theobalds Park Road and the church of St John the Baptist on the left, by the stone drinking fountain and trough. Cross the road into Flash Lane, opposite the pub. This becomes an unmetalled track leading into Whitewebbs Park, crossing a brook via the brick bridge. Pass a stile and footpath to the right, go uphill then take the next signposted footpath right. Head in the reverse direction of the arrows on two wooden posts, away from the lane at about 100°, then fork right to come to a fallen tree and adjacent tree with shattered crown. Turn right to head roughly 130° to a T-junction; turn right to head 190° then left at 125°.

Turn right at the perimeter of the golf course and follow it down on the well-defined path. Cross the meadow on the tarmac path, and take the footbridge into the next meadow. These are nature reserves, and the golf course has a number of good mature trees. Walk across the golf club car park, passing the clubhouse and take a footpath to the edge of the course indicated by yellow arrows. Cross the bridleway, following signposts, turn right over a concrete footbridge then veer right and follow a path round the edge of the pitch and putt course, returning to Clay Hill and the pub.

② Botany Bay
The Robin Hood

This is a large McMullen's roadside pub out in the country with superb views of the surrounding landscape from the huge garden at the back, which also has a weeping willow tree, plenty of seating and tables. Inside, there are two dining areas either side of the main bar, which also has a number of tables and chairs. Food is served with care and pride, 12 noon to 2.30 pm and 7 pm to 9.30 pm Monday to Saturday, and all day, 12 noon to 9 pm, on Sunday. The day's specials are chalked up, with a separate board for vegetarian dishes and desserts. Choices include home-made soups, fish courses, roasts or a very tasty goulash, all in generous portions and served with a large selection of excellent fresh vegetables – no less than seven accompanied Sunday lunch. The meals are very popular, so reserving a table is advisable, especially if you want to specify a no-smoking area. Children can eat in the restaurant areas.

Three cask ales are served: McMullen Original AK, Country Best, Special Reserve Oatmeal and Gladstone Bitter. Drinking hours are: Monday to Friday 11 am to 3 pm, 5.30 pm to 11 pm; Saturday 11 am to 11 pm; and Sunday 12 noon to 10.30 pm.

Telephone: 0181 363 3781.

How to get there: Leave Enfield on The Ridgeway (A1005), and the pub is on the left shortly after entering Botany Bay. Nearest station: Gordon Hill (BR from Moorgate), then bus 313 (not Sundays) or W8 (Sundays) or walk to The Ridgeway to join the walk.

Parking: In the large pub car park, or the overflow on the left (facing the pub), but do ask first.

Length of the walk: 4 miles. Map: OS Pathfinder 1140 (inn GR 296991).

This walk is a rural one, along pathways with sweeping vistas of open country and then, in contrast, through well-wooded Trent Country Park, once part of the Chase. It ends with a visit to a working farm.

The Walk

Leave the pub and turn left to walk along The Ridgeway through Botany Bay. The village developed after Enfield Chase was enclosed in the late 18th century, so isolated that it was named after the penal settlement as a Victorian joke. Henry Mayhew (1812–1887), novelist and co-founder of *Punch*, was one of its early residents. Pass a row of characterful humble cottages, and then some less humble semi-detached houses.

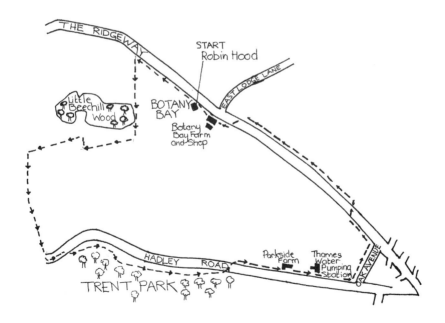

The 'Silver Jubilee' footpath.

A little way outside the village, turn left onto a signposted public footpath over two low stiles. The broad path runs gently downhill between a fence and, on the right, a row of trees, predominantly oak, and mixed shrubbery including hawthorn, blackberry and elderberry. A stone states that the path was constructed to mark the Silver Jubilee in 1977. To the left there are fine views of open countryside, with Enfield and its prominent church spire in the distance, and beyond it the high rise buildings of London.

The path skirts Little Beechill Wood on the right. Follow it over a wooden footbridge and then as it turns sharp right. On the right is a wattle fence with newly planted hawthorn in front – a traditional way of making hedges. Hawthorn also attracts a variety of birds which use it for nesting and roosting in spring and feed on the berries in autumn. Eventually the path bends right and then left to skirt a field which may contain grazing dairy cattle. At the end of this, turn left onto the public footpath to Hadley Road (don't continue straight on through the kissing-gate). After crossing a wooden footbridge, and a field of maize on the right, cross a stile to emerge onto Hadley Road, opposite an obelisk. Turn left and cross over to the right-hand side.

At the beginning of the wooded area turn right into Trent Country Park via a wooden footbridge and kissing-gate. Immediately after the gate, head left through the wood, to the left of a large oak tree. Keep left at the fork and then turn left onto a wide path. At the next fork bear left (marked with a white arrow). At the crossroads, where there is a plan of the park, continue straight ahead passing a car park on the right and toilets on the left. Cross two more crossroads, close to one another and with taps next to them. After the second crossroads go around a wooden horse stop, cross over a bridlepath and continue ahead. Pass the bridlepath exit to Hadley Road on the left and continue ahead.

At the bench, where the main path curves right, take the narrow path to the left. At the junction with the bridlepath turn right, then immediately left. Cross the stile and footbridge to Hadley Road. Turn right, cross over the road and continue ahead, passing Parkside Farm.

Turn left onto Oak Avenue and at the end turn left onto The Ridgeway. At the Royal Chace [sic] Hotel, where the pavement ends, cross the road carefully onto the opposite pavement. The road is busy but there are pleasant rural views on both sides. On an oak tree on the left, a small cross and flowers are in memory of John Timothy Codd, who died here on 9th September 1989, aged 29. Continue along the road to the Botany Bay sign on the left.

Just beyond here is the drive to the Botany Bay Farm and Shop, and a café which is open at weekends. You are invited to walk around the farm; the barns behind the shop accommodate sheep, lambs, pigs, working horses and rheas and peacocks. Leave the farm and turn left to return to the pub.

3 Arkley
The Arkley

This is a very popular family-friendly pub on the edge of Chipping Barnet, with a welcoming atmosphere, plenty of comfortable seating areas where children can eat with their parents, and a children's menu. There is a conservatory restaurant, and dining tables on a shaded patio. Lunch is served every day, 12 noon to 3 pm, and evening meals 7 pm to 10 pm (7 pm to 9 pm Sunday). Daily specials complement a fixed menu, providing interesting starters, good home-made favourites such as steak and kidney pie, fisherman's pie, fish courses, grills and platters, as well as a good choice of imaginative vegetarian dishes, traditional Sunday lunches and the occasional summer barbecue. Main courses come with good portions of fresh vegetables and the tempting home-made desserts are served with a choice of real cream, ice cream or custard. Portion sizes are generous – our order for a third course was met with genuine surprise as we indefatigably researched on your behalf. Bar snacks and liberally sized ploughman's lunches are also available.

Ind Coope Burton Bitter, Tetley Bitter and Benskins Best beers and Addlestone's cask-conditioned cider are stocked, together with a full range of bottled beers, lagers and wines. The opening hours are: Monday to Saturday 11 am to 11 pm, and Sunday 12 noon to 10.30 pm. The

restaurant is occasionally booked for private functions, mainly in the evening, so do call ahead if you're relying on a good meal.
Telephone: 0181 449 3862.

How to get there: Turn left off Barnet Hill just before the High Street onto Wood Street (A411). The pub is at the junction of Galley Lane and Barnet Road. Nearest station: High Barnet (Northern line), then bus 307 (to its terminus) or 107.

Parking: In the pub car park.

Length of the walk: 2¾ miles. Map: OS Pathfinder 1140 (inn GR 233964).

Arkley straddles the A411 to the south-west of Barnet near the site of Watling Street, the Roman road which once linked London to the north-west via Verulamium (present day St Albans). Arkley developed after the opening of East Barnet and High Barnet stations on the Great Northern Railway. It's a green belt area with many livery stables and riding schools.
This is a rural walk across fields and along tree-fringed bridlepaths to the north of the busy A411. It entails crossing a ditch and climbing over a wooden fence and a metal gate so may not be suitable for the infirm. However, it's a short walk so suitable for small children who can be lifted if necessary. In wet weather the paths become very muddy.

The Walk
Leave the pub and turn left; on the traffic island in the middle of Barnet Road/Wood Street is a newly restored parish marker on the boundary between the parishes of Arkley and Chipping Barnet.

Turn left into Galley Lane. Walk along the right-hand side. This a quiet thoroughfare where horses and riders usually outnumber cars. After the houses, pass a playing field on the right and beyond here look out for great tits and blue tits flitting about in the trees and hedgerow. Pass the entrance to the Poor Clare Monastery on the left. The order of Poor Clares was founded by St Francis and St Clare in the early 13th century. It is the strictest order of the Roman Catholic Church, with very stringent restrictions on personal and even communal property. Paradoxically, St Clare is the patron saint of television.

Homestead Farm and the Barnet Riding Centre are next door to the monastery. A little way beyond here look for a public footpath sign on the left. Take this path by crossing a ditch and climbing a (rickety) fence into a field where horse jumps may be set up. Head off half-right, then walk along the right-hand side of the field. Exit the field by the gate at the top right, turn left, and climb the facing metal gate.

Turn right and follow the hedge on the right to the end of the field.

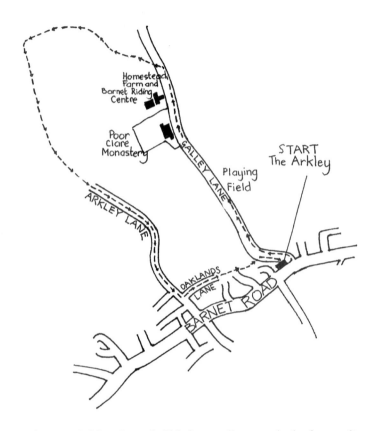

Enter the next field and veer half-left to walk towards the four radio masts ahead. Go through a break in the trees and hedge, and head across the next field (aiming to the left of the masts) to a gate and stile by the public footpath sign under a large oak tree in the hedgerow.

Cross the stile and follow the public footpath to Arkley Lane as it veers left. The narrow path cuts through high grass which attracts butterflies, including the common blue. Pass, but do not cross, a concrete footbridge over a reed-fringed stream on the right. Moorhens can sometimes be spotted here. Follow the path around to the left. It is now fringed by a variety of trees and shrubs.

Cross over the railway sleepers, walk to the end of the path and continue along Arkley Lane. The lane, flanked by detached houses with large gardens, goes gradually uphill. Shortly after it levels out, turn left onto Oaklands Lane and continue ahead when it becomes a bridlepath. At Galley Lane turn right to return to the pub.

Stanmore
The Vine

4

This traditional Sedgwick pub, with a rural setting in a conservation zone, offers a friendly welcome to strangers and regulars alike. The interior resembles a country house, with an elegant dining room (where children are welcome) overlooking the garden, a carpeted and wallpapered comfortable lounge bar, and a wooden-floored public bar.

Food is a strong point at the Vine; serving hours are 12 noon to 2.30 pm Monday to Saturday, 5.30 pm to 8 pm Monday to Friday and 12.30 pm to 2.30 pm Sunday. A menu changed daily includes such items as home-made potato and leek soup and other starters, seven choices of hot main course and tempting desserts. The food is cooked with imagination – even a simple dish like bangers and mash is enlivened with an onion sauce – and care; the main courses are accompanied by excellent fresh seasonal vegetables. Light snacks, salads, jacket potatoes and filled baguettes are also available, and tea and coffee are served all day.

Benskins Best Bitter, Tetley Bitter, Ind Coope Burton Ale and John Bull ales are served, 11 am to 11 pm Monday to Saturday, and 12 noon to 10.30 pm Sunday.

Telephone: 0181 954 4676.

How to get there: The pub is at the top of Stanmore Hill, the A410 leading north out of Stanmore, at the junction with the lane leading to Little Common. Nearest station: Stanmore (Jubilee line), then bus 142 to the pub, or turn left from the station onto London Road, turn right onto Dennis Lane and walk through Stanmore Country Park (see the last paragraph of The Walk).

Parking: There are only a few spaces by the pub but there is a public car park for Stanmore Common on Warren Lane.

Length of the walk: 3½ miles. Map: OS Pathfinder 1139 (inn GR 163931).

The walk starts among the cottages and other houses of the Little Common conservation zone, before going on to Stanmore Common, a wood right on the Middlesex boundary and very rural in atmosphere, despite its closeness to the M1. Finally, you walk round part of Stanmore Country Park, an important wildlife habitat and broadleaf woodland, as well as a fairly well-kept local secret.

The Walk

Leave the pub and turn left to walk up Little Common by the side of the pub, then between cottages to reach the green in this pleasant conservation area. It is based on what were once stables and ancillary buildings to Stanmore Hall (visible to the right), built in 1843. It did contain work by William Morris, but following a bad fire in 1979 it has been refurbished as offices. Turn half-left onto the green, follow the line of cottages on the left, then at the end walk through the barrier to face the rugby grounds. Turn left, walk just past the end of the field, turn right at the young oaks and follow the path down the side of the pitch.

Pass a post and yellow arrow pointing straight on, and reach a large, peaceful pond on the left. Follow its bank round back to a corner of the playing field – turn left between the ponds, then fork right past the cricket pitch. Cross the road, going half-left to follow a path. Keep left, pass through an oak glade and cross a tarmac path. Continue on through the public car park, then turn right between the wooden litter bin holders onto a path heading roughly north.

Pass picnic tables on the obvious path, veer left as you enter the trees and follow the path to the north-west, crossing a ditch. Now keep heading between west and north along a complex web of paths twisting through oaks and silver birch, and the odd clearing. Head towards the sound of traffic; you should hit the perimeter of the common at Heathbourne Road, by the roundabout.

Turn right onto the bridleway covered in bark chips and marked by white posts (give way to horses and keep dogs under control on the

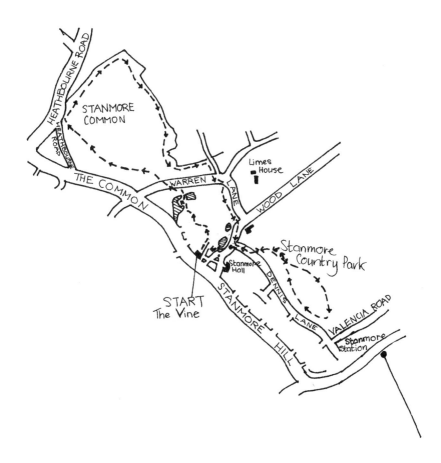

bridleway). Pass behind the house and follow the track round. This is very near the county boundary for a while, then swings round to the southeast. There is a good view over meadows to the left as the track follows a double avenue of oaks. Pass some secluded offices on the left, cross the tarmac path and continue on the track. Follow the line of the bridleway across Warren Lane – on the other side it has become too overgrown for riding.

Near Lymes (Limes) House on the opposite side of the road, turn right into the back of the rugby grounds and walk across by the trees to the left of the pitches. Leave by the gates onto Wood Lane by the Husseini Shia Islamic Centre, formerly Warren House, a Jacobean Revival mansion. Go down Dennis Lane. Just after the drive to No 63, turn left and go through a wooden kissing-gate into Stanmore Country Park, a 51 hectare conservation site, designated in 1976 but shown on very few maps. It is roughly L-shaped, to the east of Dennis Lane and north of Valencia Road/Glanleam Road.

The walk shows you the range of habitats in the park. Follow the almost overgrown path through a copse to a clearing; the back of the Islamic Centre is up on the left. You might see an urban fox in the fields here. Turn right to head south downhill, enter a small meadow and climb again to get a view over London, including the BT Tower. The path skirts the meadow, heading roughly south-east. Pass a wooden post with an arrow pointing in the reverse direction. Follow a path to the half-left, then pass more arrows pointing the way you're going. Turn right at a T-junction to head 150°, and cross the plank bridge over the stream. Take the right fork – this soon leads to another access point to the park near the junction of Valencia Road and Dennis Lane; blocks of redbrick flats overlook the meadow area.

(Start here if you came on foot from Stanmore station.) Follow the path to reed-filled ponds, drop down to the pond bank at a wooden jetty and follow this to the right to reach the stream. Turn right and cross the stream by one of the sets of stepping stones. Go back into the trees on the almost overgrown path. This leads alongside the stream back to the plank bridge. Now head 350° up a small path through pedunculate oak, birch and maples. Turn right at a larger path by a felled tree and stump cut into the shape of a seat. Turn right, go across the clearing and return to Dennis Lane. Turn right uphill, then left into Wood Lane. Turn right to pass the pond and reach the edge of the green, then return to the pub down Little Common.

Pinner
5 The Hand-in-Hand

Suburban Pinner still retains a village High Street. Halfway down from the church, the Hand-in-Hand façade has been restored to resemble the old-style shop fronts of a family grocer's and a dairy, either side of a passageway to the courtyard. On one side are bars, the converted barn at the back is an atmospheric flagstoned restaurant, and the open courtyard is an excellent spot for a quiet drink, a snack or a full meal.

This is a Whitbread Chilton inn, serving food all week. A good choice of food is available from a fixed menu and the blackboard showing the day's specials. Typical tempting fare includes a soup, freshly grilled red meat or salmon steaks, a pasta dish, at least a couple of vegetarian main dishes, salads, sandwiches and filled jacket potatoes. Traditional puddings and custard, or ice cream, and coffee or tea complete your meal. Food is served 12 noon to 8 pm Monday to Thursday, and 12 noon to 7 pm Friday and Saturday; traditional Sunday lunch is served 12 noon to 3 pm, then the usual menu is available until 7 pm. Order your food at the counter in the restaurant. Children are welcome in the restaurant.

Up to nine cask ales are kept, including Wadworth 6X, Greene King, Boddingtons Bitter, Flowers Original and Theakston XB on handpump, and four casks on a rack behind the bar dispensing the likes of Fuller's

London Pride and Old Speckled Hen by gravity. The usual range of bottled lagers and other drinks is stocked, and there is a choice of wines which may be ordered by the glass – a nice feature. Drinking times are: Monday to Saturday 11 am to 11 pm, and 12 noon to 10.30 pm on Sunday.
Telephone: 0181 866 2521.

How to get there: The pub is at 36–40 Pinner High Street (on the south side), just off the A404 (variously called Pinner Road, Marsh Road and Bridge Street here), very near Pinner station (Metropolitan line).

Parking: There is no pub car park, but there is a long-stay pay car park by the station, part of the Sainsbury's complex. There is also a free car park at Headstone Manor Heritage Centre, on the walk route.

Length of the walk: 5 miles. Maps: OS Pathfinder 1158 and 1139 (inn GR 123896).

From the wonderfully picturesque ancient village at the centre of suburban Pinner, you walk past the last resting place of Nelson's daughter and a group of fine half-timbered buildings. Continuing through open fields, part of a working dairy farm, you reach an unexpected treasure: a giant tithe barn and moated manor house. You return via Pinner's parish church.

The Walk

Leave the pub and cross the High Street. The Queen's Head opposite is just one of several timber-framed buildings surviving from medieval Pinner. Behind you, the buildings (and chimney) just downhill from the Hand-in-Hand are worth a look. Immediately beyond No 25, turn right into the alleyway Bishop's Walk. Pass Marks & Spencer, turn left at the car park, and follow the footpath to Love Lane. Turn right at St Luke's RC church, a twin-towered 1957 brick building with a stone relief of St Luke on the front. Continue into Avenue Road, to the right of the Methodist church, turn right and walk straight up Leighton Avenue.

At the top, cross Paines Lane and enter the small cemetery. A little way up the central path, just before a clump of trees and about 8 yards to the right, the railing-enclosed slab marks the grave of Horatia Nelson Ward, Nelson's natural daughter by Emma Hamilton. Horatia married Pinner's curate.

Leave the cemetery, turn right and continue along Paines Lane over the river Pinn – here merely a stream in a concrete course. Immediately after, turn right onto an unsignposted footpath emerging onto Moss Lane, opposite a Heath Robinson house (owned by, not designed by). Turn right and follow the lane round. Beyond No 96, there is a fine collection of

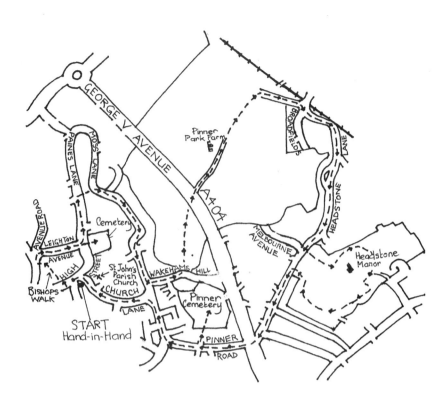

medieval buildings. Tudor Cottage has apparently been heavily restored, but East End Farm Cottage is a half-timbered building with parts dating back to the 15th century. East End House is a brick 18th-century building; the wooden barns are also of some interest.

Continue along Moss Lane and turn left into Wakehams Hill, then left again onto the public footpath signposted 'George V Avenue'. Go through the kissing-gate and you have a fine view over open fields. Follow the obvious footpath at the edge of the field to the busy main road, crossing it with care, then follow the public bridleway signposted to Headstone Lane. This is metalled to Hall's Pinner Park Farm, then continues as a track. Look to the right for a glimpse of Harrow-on-the-Hill. At the sports club gateway turn right onto the road, signposted 'Headstone Lane and Station'. At the station, turn right onto Headstone Lane and follow it round, going past Broadfields. Opposite Melbourne Avenue, turn left into the grounds of Headstone Manor.

Follow the tarmac avenue and cross the Yeading brook nearly halfway down the tennis courts on the left. At the end turn left, passing the courts

The grave of Horatia, Lord Nelson's daughter, in Pinner cemetery.

on the left, then the rear of the tithe barn on the right. Keep turning right to circle the moat. The water and the banks provide a habitat for many types of wild plants, especially elm scrub. The third side of the moat is a cobbled path by the car park; at the end, turn right into the courtyard.

You now have the rare sight of a moated manor house, parts of which date back to the 14th century, and a very fine 16th-century tithe barn. Near you on your right is the Small Barn, a contemporary of the tithe barn. To the left is the Granary, originally on Pinner Park Farm, then re-erected here and reopened in 1992. The land was originally a working farm owned by the Archbishops of Canterbury until it was 'acquired' by Henry VIII in 1545, to be passed on to a favourite. It is now owned by the Borough of Harrow, who at the time of writing are restoring the manor house. The barn houses a small museum, a café and toilets. Admission to the buildings is free, Wednesday to Friday 12.30 pm to 5 pm, Saturday, Sunday and bank holidays 10.30 am to 5 pm. A nature trail booklet on sale in the barn gives details of the surrounding flora and fauna.

After visiting the buildings, leave the courtyard between the tithe barn and granary, turn left, passing a play area on the right, and cross the brook. There is a good view of Harrow-on-the-Hill from here. Turn left to follow the Yeading brook round the edge of the field, past the weeping willows and the rich brook habitat. Bear right to follow the field boundary – the small area of woodland on the left is a remnant of the ancient forest that once covered most of Middlesex. Join the tarmac path and follow it until the stream disappears into a culvert. Turn right, following the edge of the field all the way round, to turn right again. Pass behind the pavilion, turn left onto a footpath and leave the grounds, turning left onto Headstone Lane.

Cross over George V Avenue into Pinner Road. A short way along here is the entrance to Pinner Cemetery, a tranquil, cool place even on a hot afternoon. It contains one oddity – a red granite headstone in the shape of an armchair (left of the main path a little beyond the chapel). Continue along Pinner Road, turn right up Nower Hill, then left at the green with the drinking fountain into Church Lane.

St John's parish church appears on the right, with the remarkable 1809 Loudon memorial in the churchyard. Enter by the lychgate and pass the memorial; the stone coffin shape above the arch is only ornamentation, there is a burial vault below. Parts of the church are 14th-century, the tower is 15th-century. If the church is open, explore the interior; opposite the entrance, the font has a modern elaborately carved wooden cover. Leave the churchyard by the west end. To the right is a late Georgian building once owned by the proprietor of the Queen's Head, but the Victorian extension was once the Cocoa Tree Temperance Tavern. Turn left onto High Street, pass the 17th-century wine bar and return to the pub.

Harrow Weald
The Case is Altered

This is a long-established and very popular pub with a wonderful location next to a local beauty spot. The name is said to date from the Peninsular Wars, a soldiers' corruption of Casa Alta, high house, because of its position. There is another Case is Altered in Eastcote, about 280 ft lower down, but maybe that's an altered case.

Inside, there's an older part with wooden panelling and floorboards, and a newer carpeted extension, giving a number of separate rooms with tables and seating, including a no-smoking area. The friendly bar plays host to a mixed clientele enjoying the Tetley Bitter, Ind Coope Burton Ale, Marston's Pedigree, Benskins Bitter and Harvest Ale. A wine list is chalked up.

At the back is an enormous sloping garden, where you can bring dogs on leashes, and unleash children on the good extensive play area. On a sunny day this is a perfect place to enjoy the excellent lunches served every day, 12 noon to 2 pm, or the occasional evening barbecue. There's an imaginative choice of hot daily specials, including a couple of vegetarian choices and a children's menu. The hot meals and cold snacks, such as filled rolls and ploughman's lunches, are all served in very generous portions, but there are some very tempting desserts, coffee, and cheese and biscuits.

Opening times are: Monday to Saturday 11 am to 11 pm, and Sunday 12 noon to 10.30 pm.

Telephone: 0181 954 1002.

How to get there: The pub is on Old Redding, Harrow Weald, left off Brookshill (A409) heading uphill. Nearest stations: Stanmore (Jubilee line), then walk to The Broadway for bus 340 to the foot of Clamp Hill; or Edgware (Northern line) then bus 340; or Hatch End (BR) which is near part of the walk.

Parking: You can park at the nearby car park, viewpoint and picnic area just beyond the pub.

Length of the walk: 3 miles. Map: OS Pathfinder 1139 (inn GR 145926).

The walk gives a splendid view from Old Redding, then takes you through wooded Harrow Weald Common, past Grim's Dyke Hotel, where W. S. Gilbert lived and died, and Grim's Ditch itself, an ancient earthwork, returning via a golf course and fields – a fairly easy path with no special difficulties and only one stile.

The Walk

Leave the pub, turn left and enter the car park on the left to enjoy the panoramic view of Harrow-on-the-Hill, ahead and to the left. Leave the car park, cross the road and take the public footpath opposite the car park entrance. The old pump shelter was once the water supply for an isolated group of workers' cottages, ironically called The City, for the adjacent brickworks (The Kiln). The path now taking you through the City Open Space was a former trackway in The City. At the fork turn right, go ahead to the main path, turn left onto it (not onto the parallel bridleway marked in white) and follow it round to the left to a gate across the private drive and a lodge.

Turn left onto a fairly well-defined track initially heading 190°, then following the fence, crossing small bridges. At the third plank bridge turn right through a break in the holly to walk west between rhododendron bushes. Note the magnificent redwood tree on the left. Cross over the tarmac road beside the brick wall, or make a short detour to the right to see Grim's Dyke, now a hotel, an elaborate neo-Tudor house built 1870–72 by Norman Shaw for an artist but better known as W. S. Gilbert's house from 1890 until his death in 1911.

Resume the walk through the rich and varied understorey of the wood, heading about 240°. Pass two more impressive redwood trees on the right and between two sections of tree trunk on the ground. The path twists and turns through a clump of silver birches, then past a clearing amidst tall fir

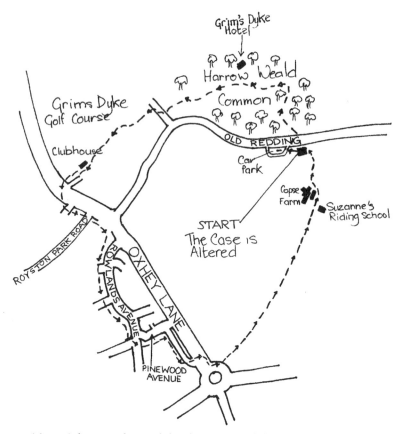

trees. Turn right over the earth bank onto a path heading 310°, waymarked by yellow arrows indicating the opposite direction. Follow this path until it swings left and at the next post (which is devoid of arrows) turn half-right, just to the right of the large tree ahead, into the thick wood. Turn left at the next post, passing the marshy pool on your right.

This is Grimsdyke lake, where W. S. Gilbert died attempting to assist a visitor who had fallen in. It is now a haven for insects and birds. The path leaves the pool and crosses two plank bridges; turn right onto the tarmac drive (by the iron gate barring unauthorised vehicles). Turn left onto a well-defined path lined by tall beeches. Pass across Grim's Ditch, originally a Saxon boundary marker, then at the fence turn left following the arrow. Turn right onto the gravel drive, still following the yellow arrows.

Turn left onto Grims Dyke Golf Course and walk ahead half-left (ignore the arrow pointing right) at about 210° to a line of bushes and

Grimsdyke, once W. S. Gilbert's home.

trees, following this on your left – this is a public right of way, but dogs should be on leashes. At the end, walk to the next line of trees and bushes and walk down this at 240° with the hedge on your left and a line of saplings on your right, to the end, by a drinking fountain on the left. Turn left to detour around the 9th green, then turn right to walk around a clump of cypress trees. Walk in front of the club house to a driveway. Walk along here to Oxhey Lane, turn left and cross over the road to the pavement.

Walk straight ahead and after the roundabout, take the first turning right onto Rowlands Avenue and walk along the pavement on the left side. Pass the end of Saddlers Close on the right and after Sequoia Park on the left, turn left onto Pinewood Avenue, and then right onto the road parallel to the main Oxhey Lane. At the end exit onto Oxhey Lane and continue in the same direction. Cross over to the left, just before the roundabout, and take the public footpath to Uxbridge Road and Brooks Hill. Go up the slope, through the kissing-gate, then continue straight on up and through a gate. As you continue through the next field there are wonderful views behind you. Cross the stile and continue ahead to Copse Farm and Suzanne's Riding School. Continue ahead to return to the pub.

7 Kingsbury
J J Moons

This pub is part of the celebrated J. D. Weatherspoon freehouse chain that turns flagging high street shops into Edwardian-style drinking palaces, full of wooden panelling, engraved glass, seating, and frequently with 'Moon' in the name. Food is featured as much as their beers and wines. Making the most of a narrow site, J J Moons has a long bar with traditional brass rail, a line of partitioned booths with tables, and at the back an area furnished to resemble a library and a no-smoking section.

Food is available from 11 am to 10 pm (12 noon to 9.30 pm on Sunday) from the usual extensive Weatherspoon menu which ranges from starters (sometimes surprisingly substantial) through varieties of burgers and jacket potatoes to interesting house specialities such as chicken with cashew nuts, sausage hotpot and steak in red wine, with additional daily specials (including traditional roast on Sunday) and tempting desserts.

Drinking hours are: Monday to Friday 11 am to 3 pm, 5.30 pm to 11 pm; Saturday 11 am to 11 pm; and Sunday 12 noon to 10.30 pm. Five beers are usually served from handpumps: Courage Directors, Youngers Scotch Bitter, Theakston Best and XB, plus a frequently changing guest beer, but ten pumps are available and during special events up to 30 beers can be racked and ready to go, to take their turn on the pumps. Because of the nature of their sites, Weatherspoon's are 'over 21' houses, so make this an adults-only walk.

Telephone: 0181 204 9675.

How to get there: The pub is at 553 Kingsbury Road, which leaves the A5 about 1 mile north of Staples Corner, and is near the junction with Fryent Way (A4140). Nearest station: Kingsbury (Jubilee line).

Parking: No pub car park! You may find parking in the vicinity of Roe Green Park, a little along Kingsbury Road, and there is a car park for Barn Hill Open Space (on Fryent Way) on the walk.

Length of the walk: 3¼ miles. Maps: OS Pathfinder 1158 (mostly) and 1159 (inn GR 193887).

Just north of Wembley is a large expanse of green open space; Fryent Country Park, primarily meadows and preserved hedgerows, was formerly farmland. The adjacent Barn Hill has attractive wooded slopes and at 280 ft, gives good views. The walk up is a little steep, otherwise the route is not strenuous or difficult – some parts may be muddy after rain. A perfect walk for spring or early summer when the meadow plants flower, birds are nesting, tadpoles swim in the ponds and humans fly kites from the hills in Fryent Park.

The Walk

Turn right from the pub onto Kingsbury Road. Cross it at the pelican crossing, then turn left into Manor Close and right into Sutherland Court. Enter Roe Green Park, following the line of trees along the road as it veers left. Turn right onto a grassy path through the 'Nature Area', a stand of young trees and grass allowed to grow long to provide a habitat for insects and birds.

Walk towards the redbrick Manor House, now council offices, then follow its fence to the right and then left. Go down the drive to the house; at the end is Roe Green Walled Garden, a conservation area not normally open to the public, but you can see it through the gate and you might be lucky – they have occasional open days. Go back down the drive and turn left onto the tarmac drive. Pass the veterans' club on the left, then a line of mature oaks on the right, with a sports ground on the left – now head half-right across the grass (about 100°) aiming for the long grassy bank to the right of the school in front. When you draw level with the south fence of the school, follow a tarmac path to the half-right to the corner of the park, at the crossroads.

Cross Kingsbury Road and go down Slough Lane, passing a couple of thatched cottages, evidence of the former rural nature of this area. Keep on

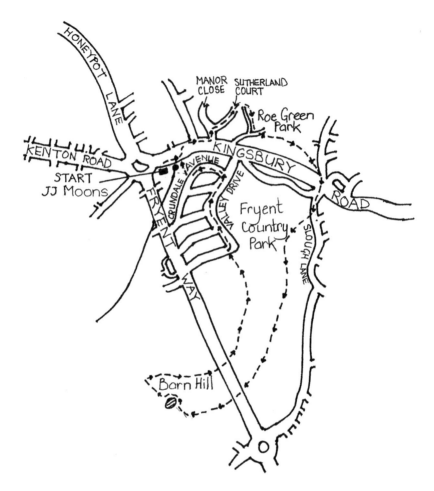

Slough Lane, to the left of the pub, passing another thatched cottage (No 142). Opposite No 134, turn right onto a public footpath signposted to Valley Drive (not into the drive immediately to the right into the school grounds).

The tarmac footpath takes you into Fryent Country Park. Follow it round to the left, skirting some stables and the marshy, reeded Oldefielde Grove ponds. When the tarmac path veers left towards stables, continue straight on along the grassy path, at the edge of the open space. Pass the fenced-off Bush Farm Orchard, which is being replanted with old varieties of fruit trees (some from seed collected from the nearby hedges). Do not follow the track to leave the open space here, but turn right and then left to follow the fence at the edge. Ahead is Bush Hill and to the right is a view of Harrow-on-the-Hill.

At an intersection of hedges, keep straight on, heading about 210° and slightly away from a hedge on your left, to head through a break in a hedge by an oak tree. Continue uphill across the meadow half-right towards an oak tree, heading about 220°. Past the tree, turn right at the path by the wooden bench at the top of the rise (to head 250°) and follow it to the road, ending between two sturdy wooden posts. Carefully cross Fryent Way and go up the opposite grass footpath, passing a wooden bench, then to the right of a tall oak tree at about 255°.

Continue along a pleasant poplar avenue, heading up Barn Hill. At the end keep straight on, veering left round a clump of oaks. At another path, go right to reach the pond at the top. Just over to the left, near the triangulation point, there is an excellent view of Wembley Stadium.

Return to the pond and follow the gravel path round the right bank. This was originally a fishpond, laid out by Humphrey Repton. He planted the surrounding woodland in 1793 when Wembley Park was being landscaped, but Barn Hill is almost all that remains of the park. At the north end of the pond, pass a tree carrying nesting boxes and the end of one path; take the next path downhill on the right, heading about 10°, which gives a fine view. Turn right to skirt a marshy, reeded depression on the right, then turn left at the next main path going downhill between oaks.

View of Barn Hill at Fryent Country Park.

Enter the open meadow, the old name of which is Upper Hydes, following the hedge on the left to the end of the field. Turn right at the ponds at the bottom, with the larger on your left; head east with a hedge on the left. Pass the end of a ditch, turn right and walk up this narrow field, which has thick clumps of shrubs as hedges. Pass a wooden bench on the left, and at the top turn left into the car park. As you do this you pass the route of Hell Lane, an ancient trackway which became disused as long ago as 1619. The hedge marked the boundary between the parishes of Harrow and Kingsbury.

Leave the car park, cross Fryent Way to reach the opposite layby, then follow the footpath into the open space. Head half-left by the hedge towards Gotford Hill. Pass to the left of a pond by a bench into the next field. Follow the path immediately to the right of the hedge as it veers left and round the edge of the field, gradually going uphill. The hedges here are remnants of the ancient forest and contain hazel, woodland hawthorn and wild service tree. Wildlife abounds in them.

Keep heading uphill from here through breaks in hedges, and pass to the left of a bench to reach the top of the hill. Admire the view from the top, and head down at about 340°, aiming for the end of a hedge and an oak tree. Turn half-left and leave the open space by the footpath. Turn right onto Valley Drive, take the fourth left into Crundale Avenue, then turn right onto the footpath between Nos 43 and 45. Turn left at the end, then right to reach Kingsbury Road. Turn left to return to the pub.

Eastcote
The Case is Altered

This very popular pub is tucked away off Eastcote High Road behind a large front garden (next to Eastcote Cricket Club ground) which acts as a glorious sun trap and is well supplied with tables and umbrellas. There is more seating and a children's play area round the back. The interior has flagstone floors in both the bars (over 21s only) and the half-timbered restaurant extension at the side. On weekdays, from 12 noon to 2.30 pm, the busy kitchen produces hot daily special dishes, as well as filled jacket potatoes, toasted sandwiches and ploughman's lunches. On Sunday, a good roast lunch is served 12 noon to 2 pm, together with a choice of other hot meals, such as a vegetarian curry, scampi and lasagne, and a range of desserts. Ales served are Ind Coope Benskins Best Bitter, Burton Ale, Tetley Bitter and Young's Special and a couple of guest beers.

In summer, the pub is open all day every day, otherwise Monday to Friday 11 am to 3 pm, 5 pm to 11 pm; and Saturday and Sunday all day.

Telephone: 0181 866 0476.

How to get there: The pub is on Southill Lane, just off the busy Eastcote High Road, B466, next to Joel Street, B472. Nearest stations: Northwood Hills or Eastcote (different branches of the Metropolitan line). Frequent bus 282 runs near the pub from either station.

Parking: In the pub car park (but please ask first); there is a public car park opposite in Eastcote House Park.

Length of the walk: 3¼ miles (but you can break off to halve this). Map: OS Pathfinder 1158 (inn GR 107890).

A gentle stroll along the banks of the river Pinn, through the grounds of a former stately home and a secret garden, returning through a remnant of ancient woodland. Part of the route may be muddy when wet. This is a particularly fine walk in spring, and definitely one for dogs.

The Walk
Leave the pub, cross the busy Eastcote High Road carefully and enter the grassland by the nearest break in the hedge. Turn left onto this strip of meadow, and follow the roadside line of trees. The thick undergrowth on your left is a haven for hedgerow wildlife. Leave the Pinn on your right till later – you're coming back that way. At Cheney Street, leave the grassland and turn right onto the road (take care – no footpath). Then a little way before the bridge turn left into the grassland, keep to the left of it, but do not leave it.

Follow a path in the grass sweeping to the right, at first between the line of trees on the left and a spinney on the right. Follow the path trodden in the grass close to the trees on the left – blackberry bushes grow in a continuous line here. The ground narrows, and when you reach a footbridge in a wooded area, turn round and come back following a well-trodden path next to the Pinn, threading its way through the trees. Look out for the wildlife thriving in the rich habitat of the river bank.

Cross the road again at the bridge. Pass just to the right of a row of pollarded trees, then keep to the left of the grassland. You are only yards away from your outward track, but the riverside atmosphere is very different. The opposite bank is completely overgrown. Birds dart across the water. Cross the river at a wooden footbridge nearly opposite where you came in. Take the gravel path leading away from the river, forking left.

This public park was once the grounds of Eastcote House, now demolished. It was owned by the Hatreys, who also owned Chequers. The parkland is studded with mature trees – about 50 species are claimed. Follow the avenue to the left of the brick wall, turn right at the top edge of the park and continue with the fence and row of trees on your left. At a flattened area and a bench, turn right and head for the end of the hedge and a pair of small iron gates. Go through these, head towards the walled garden and enter it by the gate next to the dovecote.

This isolated suntrap has the atmosphere of a secret garden, with benches for a peaceful rest. Leave through the same gate, but turn right to

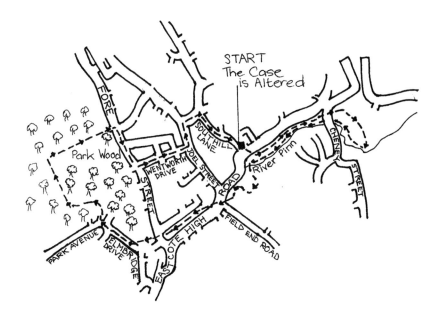

pass through the pergola and metal gate, then turn left to pass the timber-framed coach house, and cross the car park. You can shorten the walk by leaving down the car park drive; turn right at the end to return to the pub. Otherwise, head directly away from the house to join a tarmac drive and leave the park at the junction of Field End Road and Eastcote High Road.

Cross the High Road and walk towards 'Eastcote Village Conservation Area' on the right. Follow the grass by the High Road – the Old Barn House is a half-timbered building on the left. Cross the Pinn by turning right at the public footpath, then turn left to follow the track by the Pinn. Go straight across Fore Street down the public footpath, with the Pinn still on your left. Turn right at the next road, Elmbridge Drive, and where this becomes Park Avenue, just after Lovat Drive, turn right and follow the footpath sign into Park Wood.

This is ancient woodland, containing a variety of species such as oak, hornbeam and silver birch, now managed by coppicing. It also has a confusing number of paths to lead you astray. Don't panic. If you keep heading roughly north from where you came in, you're bound to hit a good straight track crossing almost exactly east-west. Turn right onto it and follow it to the edge of the wood. Just before it leaves the wood and passes between two fields, on your right are the remains of an earthwork bank that once marked the boundary of a pre-1086 hunting park.

At the end of the footpath, turn right onto Fore Street which follows the

The grounds of Eastcote House.

edge of the woodland, then, opposite the school gates, turn left onto Wentworth Drive. Turn left onto Joel Street, cross over, then walk on the grassland when the brick wall ends. Cut across the point and follow the line of trees along Southill Lane to return to the pub.

Newyears Green
The Breakspear Arms

9

A new pub with an old name: Nicholas Breakspear, in the 12th century, became the only Englishman to be elected as pope (Adrian IV). He had local connections with Breakspear House, a mile up the road. The pub has a large garden with tables and umbrellas, and the chalet-style building has a comfortable interior with plenty of dining tables, and a good range of Morland ales if all you want is a leisurely drink. These are Morland Old Masters Premium Bitter, Old Speckled Hen, Independent IPA and a frequently changing guest bitter. Beamish and Strongbow ciders are kept, as well as a range of lagers and wines. Opening times are: Monday to Saturday 11 am to 11 pm, and Sunday 12 noon to 10.30 pm.

Food is available 12 noon to 10 pm Monday to Saturday, and 12 noon to 9 pm Sunday. As well as a regular full menu, there are daily special starters and main courses, chalked up by the ordering hatch, steaks and stir-fried chicken as regular specialities, light meals and snacks, and roast lunches on Sunday. The pub goes out of its way to welcome families, with family dining tables next to children's play areas both indoors and outdoors, a children's club and videos.

Telephone: 01895 632239.

How to get there: The pub is on Breakspear Road South outside Harefield, at the junction with Breakspear Road; head north from the A40 roundabout with the B467, then fork left onto Breakspear Road South. The pub is about 1½ miles further on. Nearest station: West Ruislip (Central line); from there turn right onto Ickenham Road, left into Hill Lane, then follow the public footpath and Hillingdon Trail signs to near the pub.

Parking: In the pub car park.

Length of the walk: 3½ miles. Map: OS Pathfinder 1158 (inn GR 077880).

After walking across open fields, you go through Bayhurst Wood and Mad Bess Wood, part of Ruislip Woods and a Site of Special Scientific Interest, as mixed oak/hornbeam coppiced woods are rare. Parts of the route may be very muddy after rain and there are some awkward stiles to cross, but this is pleasant rolling countryside and the woods are birdlife havens.

The Walk
From the pub turn left, pass the end of Breakspear Road and continue on the left verge past Crows Nest Farm. Before Tile Kiln Lane on the left, there is a signposted public footpath on the right, via an almost overgrown stile in the hedge. Walk straight across the field, which may be very muddy when wet, to reach two metal gates and climb over these to cross the electric fence and barbed wire. The public footpath then continues up the left-hand side of the hedge.

At the end of the field, continue into the next one by turning right, left and right again to follow the left-hand side of the hedge. There are two squat brick towers over on the left. At the top of the field turn right – there is a small break in the barbed wire fence – then turn left and cross the metal stile by the public footpath sign. Go towards the buildings, following the track round to the left and right, keeping the buildings on your right, then leave this site heading straight on to pass stables. Go through the gate and take the track to the half-left downhill, passing a practice showjumping ground.

The drive reaches the road at a gate which is normally locked; just before this cross the stile in the fence on the right and take the path cutting off the corner of the field to the stile in the hedge by the public footpath sign. Cross this stile, which is awkwardly situated for descent above a ditch, using the signpost to steady yourself if necessary, then turn left at the road, and immediately right at the public footpath sign. Cross the stile into the field and follow the footpath, not the fenced-off bridleway, crossing stiles at a field boundary as you head towards Bayhurst Wood.

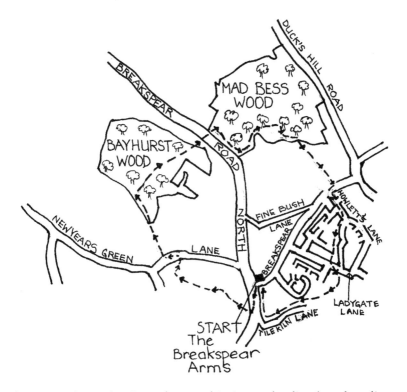

The next stile (at the time of researching) was derelict, but the adjacent metal gate is only held shut by twisted wire.

Walk briefly along the bridleway then turn left by a fencepost to enter the wood on a path following the fence to the left. At a picnic area, where some trees carry bird boxes, turn right onto a broad path. Continue straight on up (not down to the left) following a brown Hillingdon Trail (HT) sign. This is a pleasant broadleaf wood, a relic of prehistoric Middlesex woodland with many characteristic coppiced hornbeam stools, oaks, silver birch and beech, as well as a rich birdlife, including jays, nuthatches, blue tits, tree creepers and woodpeckers. Pass a small toilet block and continue on the track past rangers' huts and a car park. Leave on the access road and cross Breakspear Road North to enter Mad Bess Wood.

This wood was first mentioned in 1769, but the origin of the name is an enigma. Turn right immediately on entry, following a public footpath along the side of the wood heading roughly south-east as far as the edge of the wood, then turn left at a signpost indicating three paths. Walk between trees on both sides, then with a field on your right and the wood on your

Mad Bess Wood.

left. Just inside the wood at the north corner of the field is a small area enclosed by a box privet hedge, with wooden entrance gates and a crazy paving cross on the ground. This is an open air Scout chapel, commemorating Ruislip youth killed in the Second World War. Continue east, passing another three-way signpost along a well-defined gravel path. Ignore a first public footpath to the right, then turn right at the second (the sign was missing at the time of researching, but the post is there). Walk down the obvious path, turn right at the end by another public footpath signpost, then immediately left.

Leave the wood by crossing the stile into the field. Walk down with the hedge on the left, cross a stile and continue past a floodlit sports field, crossing another stile to arrive at the road. Turn right then left at the Woodman into Howlett's Lane. Pass a row of shops and the end of Wyte Leaf Close, then turn right at the HT signs and follow them through the housing estate. Turn left onto Ladygate Lane, pass the primary school, then turn right at the HT signs, following the fenced footpath between playing fields. The path is shaded by a line of poplars, then limes.

Go right where the path forks, follow the HT sign and the fence. At the start of a field, cross a stream, turn left at the HT sign, cross the field and leave it by the stile. Now ignore the brown HT sign, turn right and follow the track by the field, following this round until it meets the road. Turn right and walk along the right-hand verge to return to the pub.

⑩ Hill End, Harefield
The Plough

Harefield is blessed with very many excellent pubs in relation to its size, including the Plough just outside at Hill End. This is a freehouse on a quiet road that is everything a village pub should be, offering a friendly welcome, a good range of ales, home cooking and a (sometimes) friendly tortoiseshell cat. They are used to walkers, being on the Hillingdon Trail. The pub was built early in the 19th century, and is recorded in the 1861 census as the Plough beerhouse. The bar walls are decorated with a number of old photographs of Harefield pubs.

No less than nine cask ales are usually available, including Fuller's London Pride, Marlow Rebellion IPA, Timothy Taylor Landlord, Ruddles Best Bitter, Brakspear Bitter and Batemans XB Best and Valiant Original bitters, with changes from time to time. Stowford Press traditional Weston's cider is also kept.

Drinking hours are: Monday to Saturday 11 am to 3 pm, 5 pm to 11 pm and traditional Sunday hours. Home-cooked pub food is served at very reasonable prices and in generous portions Monday to Saturday 12 noon to 2.30 pm and 5.30 pm to 8 pm, including meat pies, scampi, sausage, gammon, home-made quiche, filled jacket potatoes, and ploughman's lunches with a wide range of cheeses. Tempting home-made desserts are

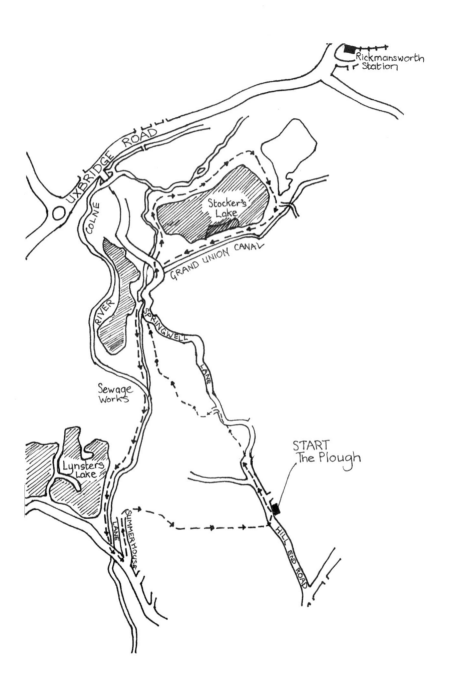

Rickmansworth Station

UXBRIDGE ROAD

Stocker's Lake

GRAND UNION CANAL

COLNE

RIVER

SPRINGWELL LANE

Sewage Works

Lynsters Lake

SUMMER HOUSE LANE

START
The Plough

HILL END ROAD

available, together with unlimited tea or coffee. Children are requested to stay in the small garden at the back. No food is served on Sundays, normally, but walkers may bring their own sandwiches; groups telephoning in advance may find that food can be organised for them.
Telephone: 01895 822129.

How to get there: The pub is on Hill End Road, Harefield, off Rickmansworth Road, past the hospital and on the right. Nearest station: Rickmansworth (Metropolitan line) and walk past the Aquadrome to the canal, joining the walk at Stocker's Lock; or Northwood (Metropolitan line) then bus 331 to Harefield Green.

Parking: There is very limited parking by the pub, and a few spaces further on by the roadside. There is a small car park at Springwell Lock and a large one at Rickmansworth Aquadrome.

Length of the walk: 3¼ or 4¾ miles. Map: OS Pathfinder 1139 (inn GR 051916).

The Colne valley provides some magnificent views early in the walk. You can then visit Stocker's Lake Nature Reserve, for which you should prepare in advance (see below), before returning via a rural section of canal towpath. Don't forget your binoculars. There are a few stiles to climb, but they are generally in good condition.

Stocker's Lake is a flooded gravel pit reserve managed by the Herts & Middlesex Wildlife Trust, which requests that you either apply in advance for a free entry permit, become a member of the Trust, or become a Friend of Stocker's Lake, to support their work. The Trust is based in St Albans, and can be contacted on 01727 858901. Stocker's Lake deserves support, as it is a magnet for waterfowl.

The Walk
Leave the pub and turn right. Follow the brown Hillingdon Trail (HT) signs along Hill End Road which becomes Springwell Lane then bends sharp right. Turn left (HT sign) through a gateway onto a drive towards a cottage, then turn right, off the drive, following an HT sign along a footpath between fencing and a hedge. Cross the stile and follow the signposted path diagonally across the field, admiring the view to the left over the Colne valley. Climb another stile at the opposite fence to use a footpath through a wooded copse.

Turn left at the road, taking care – there is no footpath. After just a few yards, turn left onto a track at Springwell Farm (HT signs). Follow the track round to the right and left and downhill. Down to the left, just behind Maple Lodge Sewage Works, there is a nature reserve, and in front

Coppermill Lock.

of it the Colne meets the canal. To the right is Springwell Reed Bed Nature Reserve, an important waterfowl habitat.

The track veers right, a path joins from the left, and you get more good views of the reed bed. The track descends; just before it becomes a private drive, turn right onto a signposted, fenced footpath. This climbs, then descends to meet the road. Turn left and carefully walk on the left down to the footpath by the cottages. Cross the canal, by the car park. This is the start of the Hillingdon Trail, whose brown arrows are useful markers in many walks in this book – it runs for 20 miles to Cranford Park by Heathrow.

You aren't going this far today; you can return now on the canal towpath (skip three paragraphs to resume [**] at Springwell Lock) or visit Stocker's Lake. To continue, go along the road, which swings away from the canal and crosses a brook. Just before a second bridge, over the Colne, turn right and pass the vehicle barrier to enter Stocker's Lake Nature Reserve.

Follow the path, to the left of the lake and the right of the river. The lake has a number of islets acting as refuges for the birds and is well screened by trees, with breaks to allow good viewing. Don't neglect the view to the left over the river. The lake has the largest heronry in Hertfordshire (37 pairs in 1992) and attracts a variety of wildfowl. Cormorants can be seen fishing from perches on the lake. Follow the edge of the lake on the gravel path to its end, continuing on an earth path and leave the nature reserve by the wooden gate.

Take a grass path to the half-right, then turn right onto a gravel path, following it between a recreational lake, Bury Lake, on the left and Stocker's Lake on the right. Keep straight on, go through the kissing-gate and turn right onto the canal towpath at Stocker's Lock.

Start here if you are coming from Rickmansworth station. Follow the towpath under the bridge, with the nature reserve on your right. There is a wartime pill box on the left, one of a number on the canal. Pass long-term moorings for houseboat owners and a large derelict building on the left to return to Springwell Lock.

[**] Stay on the towpath, cross a branch of the Colne and pass the pumping station. Walk past the reed bed nature reserve seen earlier. Cross the footbridge over the other branch of the Colne and continue past the sewage works, crossing several water channels. Another flooded gravel pit, Lynsters Lake, can be seen on the right. You approach Coppermill Lock past some impressive brick mill buildings, originally papermills but converted into coppermills at the end of the 18th century. Some are now being renovated. A sluice enables canoeists to practice whitewater slaloming – a rare sight on a canal.

Leave the towpath here and cross the canal by the narrow roadbridge. Pass the refurbished manager's house, then turn left onto Summerhouse Lane. At the end of the mill site, turn right (HT signs) towards Parkwood Farm Kennels. At the kennels, fork left onto the public footpath (HT signs). The path ascends through a broadleaf wood between ferns, blackberries and hawthorn. Cross a plank bridge; the path levels off to pass between fields. At the road turn left to return to the pub.

Harefield
Disraeli's Alehouse and Hostelry

11

Disraeli's, once called the King's Head, is now a glorious Victorian-style pub and restaurant. The traditional bar has bare floorboards, stools, an ageing sofa, a relaxed friendly atmosphere, newspapers and five cask ales: Marston's Pedigree, Whitbread Fuggles Imperial, Boddingtons, Flowers Original (one of these being rotated with various Whitbread-based beers) and Disraeli's – 'specially brewed by Courage'. There is also a full wine list. The bar is open Monday to Saturday 11 am to 11 pm; and Sunday 12 noon to 10.30 pm.

Hot and cold bar snacks are available, but we heartily recommend the restaurant, open 12 noon to 3 pm and from 7 pm, seven days a week. Meals are prepared to a high standard, most meat or fish dishes being accompanied by fine-tasting sauces and, naturally, fresh vegetables. The good-value set menu, with intriguing dishes named for Victorian personalities, offers one, two or three courses depending on your appetite and pocket, and there is an à la carte menu. The home-made desserts are delicious; two courses should suffice for most people! Telephone 48 hours ahead for their lobster or steak Wellington, or any special requests.

Breakfast is served from 8 am (9 am on Sunday) to 10.30 am, morning

coffee from 11 am and afternoon tea from 3 pm. Accommodation is also available.
Telephone: 01895 822269.

How to get there: Disraeli's is on the High Street, approaching the green from the Uxbridge direction. Nearest station: Northwood (Metropolitan line) then bus 331 to the pub.

Parking: There is a very limited amount of parking space by the pub, otherwise try to find on-street parking in Harefield. The walk passes the car park at Bayhurst Wood.

Length of the walk: 5 miles. Maps: OS Pathfinder 1139 and 1158 (inn GR 052904).

This is an almost entirely rural walk with fine views of rolling countryside and pathways through mixed woodland.

The Walk
Leave the pub and walk ahead along the High Street, passing Harefield House, now offices but a 17th-century house with a 19th-century exterior. Turn right onto Breakspear Road North, walk past the green and turn left onto Northwood Road. Walk to the end of the houses (No 160) and turn right onto a footpath running between a fence and a wood. Continue into a maize field, with the hedge on the left, up to a barbed wire fence. Cross a 'stile' into a meadow and continue ahead, keeping close to the hedge on the left. At a break in the hedge on the left, cross via a stile into the next field, used as a horse gallop, and turn right to follow the hedge. Go straight across an entrance to the field on the right via two stiles, and continue to the end of the field.

Cross a stream via a steel plate and then a stile, then veer slightly left to follow the hedge up the slope. At the end of the field turn left into the corner, cross a stile into another field, then turn right to follow the public footpath to the left of the hedge. At the end of the field cross the stile in the right-hand corner under the power lines, coming out onto a broad track. Head roughly south-east on this well-defined gravel track between tree-lined hedgerows which attract a variety of birdlife, including tits and nuthatches. Follow the path round to the right and uphill.

The track soon broadens out, passes a cottage on the left and emerges onto Jackets Lane. Continue ahead to Duck's Hill Road and turn right. At the edge of Copse Wood on the left, just before Kingfisher Close, turn left onto a bridlepath and immediately right onto a path parallel to the road. Go ahead, cross straight over a wide track and continue along the path through a wood of hornbeams and oaks. At the beginning of Mad Bess

Wood on the right, turn right, cross the road and enter the wood by a bridlepath.

Continue ahead along the obvious track marked with horsehead signs. At a good firm, stony path turn left (at 210°), cross over one path and at the next crossroads turn right onto a track wide enough for vehicles, following a Hillingdon Trail (HT) sign. At the next crossroads turn left, still following the HT sign. Follow these signs out of the wood to the road, cross over and walk up the road opposite. A little way along, turn right immediately before the car park to enter Bayhurst Wood, taking a soft bridlepath, or a footpath running parallel and to the left of it, both following the perimeter of the wood.

Rejoin the Hillingdon Trail, passing a horse barrier and then an entrance on the right to Tarleton's Lake Nature Reserve, a seasonal lake and marsh. Leave the wood towards, then under, the power lines following the path at the edge of the field. At the end of the field follow HT signs across a stile. Go through a wooded area, keeping a lookout for an HT waymarker

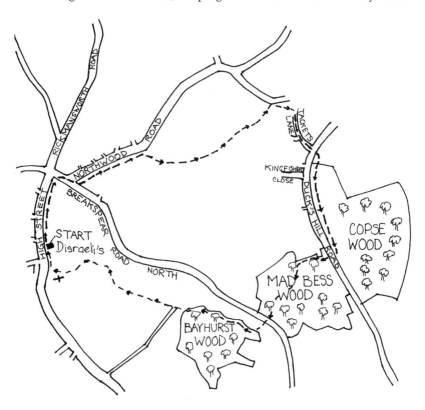

Copse Wood.

(nearly hidden by a fallen tree at the time of writing) pointing to a stile. Go over this stile and continue uphill along the right-hand edge of the field. At the top cross a stile and turn right. Climb another stile and follow the HT signs along the edge of the field, then go left at the end, downhill and cross a stile.

Veer left at the HT sign and go through a kissing-gate to pass along St Mary's churchyard wall to its end, then turn left into the churchyard. Turn right to pass the church, which is a fascinating mixture of periods, some parts dating from the 12th century, and much from the 14th. The interior is crammed with monuments. On the other side of the church is an Australian First World War military cemetery; memorial services are held on ANZAC day (25 April).

Leave the churchyard, turn right onto the tarmac road, right again at the main road and cross over. Pass 17th-century almshouses on the right, founded by Alice, Countess of Derby. Continue ahead to return to the pub.

Uxbridge
The Crown and Treaty

This historic house is named after abortive Civil War peace talks held here between Charles I and the Parliamentarians in early 1645. The king and his party entered by the front, and the Parliamentarians by the back. Each side believed it was on the verge of victory, so no peace treaty resulted. Only one wing survives of the early 17th-century Treaty House, the rest having been demolished in the 1750s.

The grounds were bought as a canal wharf site in 1802, when the building became an inn. The exterior, particularly the north side, is still reminiscent of a grand house. An upstairs room has the original 17th-century wooden panelling, removed at one time to furnish a room in the Empire State Building but returned to the UK in the 1950s. The wooden panelling, floorboards, tables and settles in the main ground floor bar give it a historical atmosphere, enhanced by the tankards hanging from the roof beam.

Good home-cooked food is served Monday to Friday 12 noon to 3 pm and 6 pm to 9 pm and Sunday 12 noon to 2.30 pm. There is a printed menu, but the daily specials chalked up are well worth investigating. These include soups, pies, beef stroganoff, a range of vegetarian choices and a number of summer salads. Our meals came with either proper home-made chips or a mixture of wild and long-grain rice – nice details. Desserts, tea and coffee are available. There is a children's menu and families are welcome inside.

Whitbread Bitter, Wethered Bitter, Old Speckled Hen, Flowers Original, Marston's Pedigree, Morland Bitter and Boddingtons Bitter are kept on handpump, and a couple of specialities are dispensed directly from casks behind the bar. Opening times are: Monday to Saturday 11 am to 11 pm; and Sunday 12 noon to 10.30 pm. On weekend evenings things can get quite lively and crowded, but there are other times when you can relax with a quiet pint in one of the numerous nooks and crannies in this piece of history.

Telephone: 01895 233891.

How to get there: The pub is on Oxford Road (A4020) leaving Uxbridge, just before the bridge over the canal. Nearest station: Uxbridge (Metropolitan and, in peak hours only, Piccadilly lines).

Parking: In the pub car park (but please ask first).

Length of the walk: 3½ miles. Map: OS Pathfinder 1158 (inn GR 052846).

This is an easy walk, nearly all on good paths beside one of three waterways: the Grand Union Canal, river Colne and Fray's River, with the Colne in particular offering many opportunities to see wildlife, a rich mix of flora and fauna occupying a waterside niche so close to a built-up area. The route is all on the flat with no stiles.

The Walk

Turn left from the pub and cross the bridge over the canal. Turn left onto the path in front of the Rank Xerox building, go through the gate and turn right onto a good metalled towpath. Pass several boats at long-term moorings; hearth and home to their hardy occupants. This canal is much wider than many other British canals, so some boats are twice the width of standard narrow boats. Cross a side-branch. A milepost states that Braunston is 82 miles away northwards, an impressive sign, literally, of the extent of this waterway.

Just before the road bridge, walk up the incline, right of the towpath, to the road and turn right onto St John's Road. Pass the end of Riverside Way on the right and then take the public footpath following the bank of a branch of the river Colne. This is easiest to see by entering the grassy area just after the bus shelter. Pass through a curtain of weeping willows, and then by a pub on the left. The trees now lining the path on both sides, and the wild land on the opposite bank, make the route a good wildlife corridor fairly near a main road.

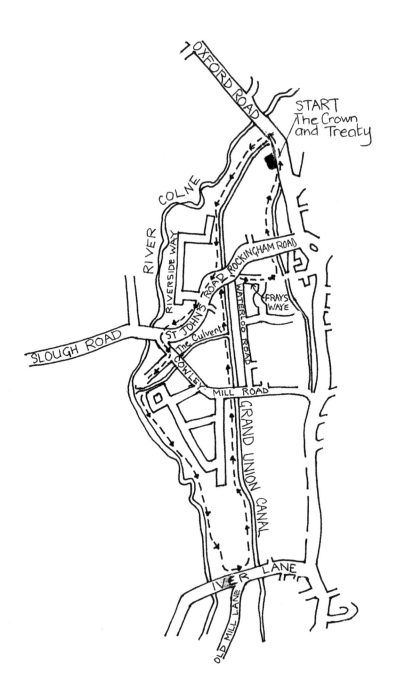

START
The Crown
and Treaty

OXFORD ROAD

RIVER COLNE

RIVERSIDE WAY

ROCKINGHAM ROAD

ST JOHN'S ROAD

WATERLOO ROAD

FRAYS WAYE

SLOUGH ROAD

The Culvert

COWLEY

MILL ROAD

GRAND UNION CANAL

IVER LANE

OLD MILL LANE

The land opposite, part of Uxbridge Moor, actually lies between two branches of the Colne. These come together near the next road bridge, where you leave the river bank, go across Slough Road before the bridge, and walk down Cowley Mill Road opposite, by the garage. Turn right into Longbridge Way by the Sportsman's Inn and keep straight on as the road becomes a track to the left of the culvert, finally becoming a public footpath signposted along the left-hand side of the culvert.

The culvert, which originates at the canal, now joins the Colne; the lack of a public bridge over this explains the detour from the Colne bank. The Colne itself divides into the main stream and the Colne brook near here – the proximity of all this water and the untended land make it a wildlife haven. Follow the path round to the left along the river bank and you are among copious wild plants, insects and birdlife; the river is a mass of rushes. Dragonflies and waterfowl abound. Cross a strip of grassland alongside the river, then go straight across a private road from a works site across a private bridge – stay on the left bank. Over to the right you can just see a flooded gravel pit, another attraction for waterfowl; you may see swans.

Leave the riverside at the brick arch road bridge, following the path round to the left to join Iver Lane. Walk along this, passing the end of Old Mill Lane on the right, then just before the canal bridge turn left and join the towpath, heading north back to Uxbridge. Pass some short- and long-

Grand Union Canal at Uxbridge.

term moorings. You may see a heron out fishing here; humans need licences. Pass under a road bridge, and the landscape is now more urban, with a row of houses on the left. Between the two covered industrial bridges keep a lookout on the left, behind a brick wall where no mooring is allowed, for a take-off from the canal which is the start of the culvert you followed earlier to the Colne.

Pass the boatyard and go under the roadbridge, still guarded by a wartime pill box. Immediately after the bridge, leave the towpath by the inclined path to the left and turn left to cross the canal by the bridge, taking Rockingham Road. Then turn right into Waterloo Road and left into Frays Waye. Keep straight on at the end across the park and turn left at Fray's River, following the path alongside leading to Rockingham Road at the bridge. Cross over and continue on the left of the river and enter Fassnidge Park. Walk through the park, heading for the north-east corner, and leave it by the gate near the start of the river culvert. Turn left at the main road, Oxford Road, and follow it round back to the pub, which contrasts strikingly with the modern office building opposite.

13 Cowley Peachey
The Turning Point

With a beautiful position right next to the canal, the pub's name refers to the winding or turning point in the pub's backyard where the widening in the canal enables 60-ft narrow boats to turn. The tables and chairs out here are a glorious suntrap in summer and you can watch canal life going by as you enjoy a leisurely drink or a meal.

There is an extensive bar menu, for outside or in the comfortable bars, and the food is good; the hot main dishes of the day are served with fresh seasonal vegetables (three plus potatoes), and usually include a vegetarian choice. The bar menu is usually available during opening hours. Summer barbecues are held on weekday lunchtimes and a couple of evenings, and if all this is not mouth-watering enough there is a separate restaurant with upmarket specialities such as poached skate wing or beef stroganoff. Children may be brought into the restaurant, but not the main bar.

Greene King IPA and Rayments Special Bitter are dispensed from handpumps, and the opening hours are: Monday to Saturday 11 am to 11 pm; and Sunday 12 noon to 4 pm, 7 pm to 10.30 pm.

Telephone: 01895 440550.

How to get there: The pub is at Canal Cottages, Packet Boat Lane, Cowley Peachey; left off the A408 (heading north) in Cowley Peachey, immediately after the canal bridge. Nearest stations: West Drayton (BR) then a short walk along the towpath to Trout Road to join the walk, or continue on to the pub; Uxbridge (Metropolitan and, peak only, Piccadilly lines) then bus 222, or take the towpath to join the walk at Iver Lane.

Parking: The pub car park can get busy – use roadside parking along Packet Boat Lane or in the industrial area on the other side of the bridge.

Length of the walk: 3 or 2½ miles. Map: OS Pathfinder 1158 (inn GR 053812).

A walk along some picturesque waterways, starting and finishing on the Grand Union Canal and with a stroll by the river Colne and a large lake.

The Walk
From the pub, cross the canal and turn right onto the towpath. Go over the arched footbridge and continue along, passing the end of the Slough Arm, a long straight branch that ends near Slough station. Either go under the associated footbridge or cross it to take the Slough Arm towpath as a pleasant short cut. You will cross Fray's River, then leave the towpath at the metal footbridge about ½ mile from the branch point (rejoin the Walk below **).

Otherwise continue straight on, passing a milepost indicating 84 miles to Braunston, a canal junction near Daventry. There are a number of houseboat moorings. These are highly sought after; Cowley Peachey is the canal equivalent of Mayfair.

At the next bridge leave the towpath, walk up to the road, turn right and cross the canal. Continue down Trout Road, follow it round to the right, crossing Fray's River, and take the left fork signposted Beeches Way Bridleway, continuing along the bridleway when the vehicle road ends. On the left, behind trees and hedges, are large expanses of water, glimpsed occasionally through gaps in the hedge but inaccessible to you as this is jealously maintained private fishing.

You now cross the Slough Arm via a metal footbridge (** rejoin the walk from the short cut here). As you cross, look to the left to see the canal itself crossing the river Colne via a short aqueduct. The path now passes through land left wild, then the river joins it on the left. Pass a small car park at the end of a lane – if you need refreshments, a small cabin just down the lane sells snacks and hot and cold drinks. Follow the path through a metal kissing-gate, staying to the right of the river – do not cross it – and you now walk between two bodies of water, the river on your left and Little Britain Lake on your right.

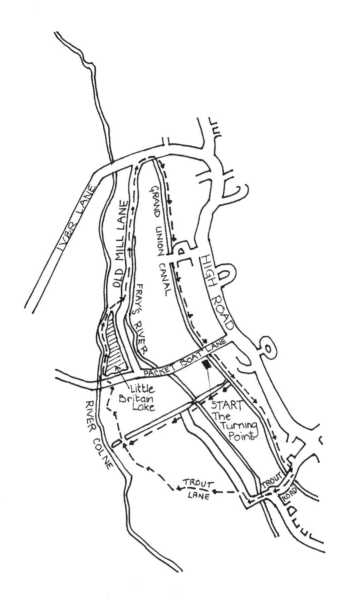

Take time to appreciate this section of the walk. There is always something special about walking with water on each side of you, and this is a peaceful shady path. The background noise from the M25 can be heard beyond the meadows to the left, like a distant waterfall, but the babbling

61

of the Colne and the calls of ducks are much closer. The river and the lake are usually lined by anglers, out for 'mainly chub in the river, and tench, roach and all sorts in the lake'. The trees lining the path and lake, and all this water, make it a good spot for birdwatching. The Colne path ends just before a weir on the left and at the end of the lake on the right.

Turn right, at the small picnic area. Walk across the grass and turn left at the road, Old Mill Lane. Walk along the grassy bank of Fray's River, as there is no footpath. Many anglers' stands line the road, especially where the Colne nearly joins the Fray. You may see a heron competing for the fish. Continue on the left as the verge ends.

Now you see where the lane gets its name – the derelict Old Mill House on the right, with Fray's River as a millrace. An old mill by the stream, but if you start singing *Nellie Dean*, you spent too long at the pub. Pass the Old Mill Farm and its shop on the left, then at the end of the lane turn right onto Iver Lane, cross the humpback bridge over the canal and turn right to join the towpath just before the lock.

(Start the walk here if you came on foot from Uxbridge.) Go past Cowley Lock and the keeper's cottage. Boat users are grateful for the fact that you can travel from here and then on the Paddington Arm and Regent's Canal without encountering another lock until Camden. Follow the towpath along the recreation area, under a low bridge, past more moorings and then leave it at the next humpback bridge to return to the pub.

Swans on the Slough Arm of the Grand Union Canal.

14 Stanwellmoor
The Anchor

This is a Morland's house in a village somewhat cut off by Heathrow airport, reservoirs and the M25, but treasured by its regulars. It is a friendly and welcoming place with a garden at the back, a large and comfortable bar, and a separate restaurant in the conservatory. Food is available in the bar and in the restaurant, which has a separate full, upmarket menu. The food is very well prepared and served with pride and care at the Anchor, as shown in details – even accompanying rolls come hot and crisp. The bar snack menu includes a range of steaks, omelette and fish cooked to order as well as a hot daily special. Excellent ploughman's lunches and sandwiches are also available, and there is a range of tempting desserts, and tea and coffee. Children may eat with their parents.

Food is served 12 noon to 3 pm and 5 pm to 10 pm Monday to Saturday, 12 noon to 3 pm Sunday. Drinking hours are: Monday to Saturday from 12 noon (note this late start) through to 11 pm; and traditional Sunday hours. Beers served are Morland Imperial, Tanners Jack, Old Speckled Hen and a changing guest beer.

Telephone: 01753 682707.

Staines Moor.

How to get there: Take Horton Road off exit 14 from the M25 (do not take the A3113) and follow this east into Stanwellmoor straight to the pub. Nearest station: Staines (BR), then bus 606 (not Sunday) from the bus station to the Anchor, or walk to Staines Moor and pick the walk up from there.

Parking: In the pub car park.

Length of the walk: 3 miles. Map: OS Pathfinder 1174 (inn GR 041748).

Stanwellmoor, practically at the end of a runway on one side and right next to the M25 on the other side, does not have a lot of through traffic. Do not be put off by the situation – the walk starts beside one of the giant reservoirs and then takes you over Staines Moor, a precious wildlife habitat and an early Site of Special Scientific Interest. You return to Stanwellmoor via the Wraysbury river and a path by the M25 embankment, a useful green corridor.

The Walk

Leave the pub and turn right, go past the post office and turn right into Hithermoor Road. The houses on the left are set back from the road behind one of the ubiquitous brooks here. Follow the road round to the

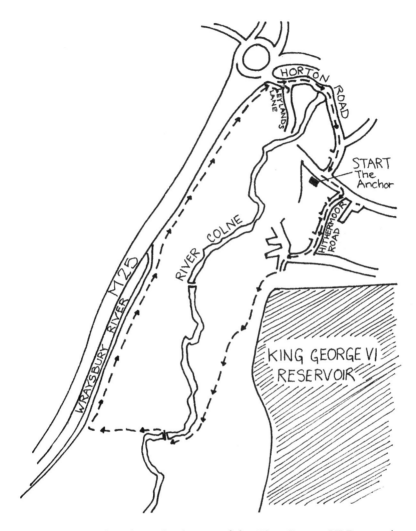

right as it approaches the embankment of the King George VI Reservoir.

Turn left onto the public footpath to Staines. Follow the concrete path round the reservoir perimeter fence. After about ⅓ mile, at the end of the field on the right, turn right off the perimeter path, through a kissing-gate, onto a grassy path signposted Colne Valley Way. Follow this round the edge of the field fenced off to the left and cross the wooden footbridge over the Bonehead Ditch to emerge onto Staines Moor.

The river to your right is the Colne; take the path following its bank. The river, its rushy banks, the moor itself, which has not been ploughed for over 1,000 years, and the nearby reservoirs make this area a haven for wildflowers, insects and waterfowl. Dragonflies can be seen flitting along the river and the undisturbed anthills are home to the yellow meadow ant. More obviously, you can see cattle and horses; registered commoners have had grazing rights since 1065.

Cross the Colne at the concrete footbridge. Turn left to follow the bank at first, then turn slightly to the right to cross a marshy depression by a gravel track and keep straight on roughly west across the moor towards the motorway. To the right is an earth mound, the remnants of the butts from a rifle range active from 1862 for 30 years – you can extend the walk slightly by climbing the butts for the view over the moor and surrounds, then returning to this track.

At the edge of the field, cross the stile and turn right to follow the track of a former railway line. It was opened in 1885 to connect Staines to the GWR at West Drayton – the rifle range on the moor was closed a few years later because of the hazard to passengers. The line was closed in 1965. The gravel path merges with a metalled road – keep on with the Wraysbury river on your left between you and the M25. This corridor of water and shrubbery is kept free from human encroachment by the motorway. The road becomes a track after a water company site, with a hedge on the right. The main course of the river disappears under the motorway, and you eventually approach a large roundabout.

Turn left from the track onto Leylands Lane, then immediately right onto Horton Road and follow it into Stanwellmoor. Pass a converted mill building straddling the former millstream, and a little further on an impressive weeping willow in the garden of a bungalow it almost covers. Follow the road round to return to the pub.

Staines
The Swan

15

The Swan is a village pub on a quiet cul-de-sac. It is set back from the road behind the common, and behind it is a beer garden and an aviary with parakeets and doves. The pub has a large, comfortable L-shaped bar and is very popular at lunchtimes with a range of customers – workers in muddy wellies cheek by jowl with office lunchers in charcoal grey suits.

Hearty unpretentious pub food is served at very reasonable prices for good-sized portions, including meals such as gammon, plaice, burgers and moussaka, as well as filled jacket potatoes, ploughman's lunches and hot and cold desserts. The ordering system is idiosyncratic – order and pay for the food at the bar and receive a playing card. Your meal is brought in to the cry of 'queen of spades' or whatever, a delicious way of being lucky at cards. The cards are dealt for lunch 12 noon to 2.30 pm Monday to Saturday and 12 noon to 2 pm Sunday, and on Monday to Friday evenings, 7 pm to 9 pm.

This Labatt's house naturally serves Labatt's Canadian-style lager, as well as Courage Best, Bass, Old Speckled Hen and one or two guest beers. The drinking hours are: Monday to Saturday 11 am to 11 pm; and Sunday 12 noon to 10.30 pm.

Telephone: 01784 465106.

How to get there: The Swan is on Moor Lane. From London, head into Staines on London Road (A308), follow the one-way system round South Street, past the bus station, and before the bridge turn right to leave on Wraysbury Road (B376), then fork right onto Moor Lane. Nearest station: Staines (BR) – the rear exit of the station is on Gresham Road, near part of the walk.

Parking: In the pub car park.

Length of the walk: 4½ miles. Map: OS Pathfinder 1174 (inn GR 027727).

Starting from the oldest part of Staines, you walk alongside the Thames and then through Shortwood Common before touching on Staines Moor. This is a pleasant walk on the flat with no stiles to cross, much of the route being beside water with a chance to see plenty of waterfowl. Do keep children under control by the water's edge and when crossing two railway lines. Some parts of the common may be muddy after rain.

The Walk

Leave the pub, turn right and walk along the common land. In this area was a Neolithic camp, possibly the oldest settlement in Staines. Go under the A30 bridge, over the reservoir aqueduct and pass the end of Annie Brookes Close to the small common. On the left is a Herdsman's Cottage (1900) erected by the Committee of Commoners. Grazing rights on Staines Moor are still managed by representatives of registered commoners, who may graze one horse or two cattle on the moor.

Just past the cottage is the local pound. Turn right at a public footpath sign, then turn left at the next path, which becomes Vicarage Road. Follow this to Wraysbury Road; at the corner on the left is Duncroft House. This was formerly a hunting lodge for an area of land that included the river bank. In 1215 the nobles who were to sign Magna Carta may have gathered here before going on to Runnymede, just a little way along the river. Cross over and continue straight on past St Mary's church.

The first stone church was built on this ancient site in 675 AD. In the 8th and 9th centuries this was the site of an important Minster for what is now south Middlesex and south Buckinghamshire. The oldest part of the present church, the bottom of the tower, dates from 1631, most of the rest from 1828.

Turn right at Church Street and, at the river, turn left to walk along the riverside path, going under Staines Bridge. Go over where the Colne joins the Thames, and just after the back of the old town hall turn left down a footpath signposted Staines Day Centre to see the freshly scrubbed splendour of what is now an Arts Centre, incorporating a café; the old town hall was built in 1880. The front is flanked by two preserved red

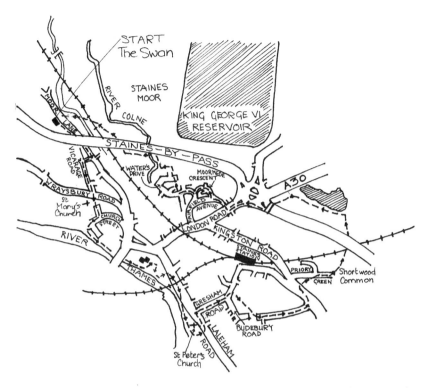

telephone boxes. Resume the riverside walk by entering the adjacent park, passing the war memorial and turn left at the river. The path now veers to the left, skirting a car park. Turn right at the road and regain the river by the railway bridge. You should see swans here, amongst other waterfowl.

Follow the Thames path to St Peter's, a substantial redbrick church built in 1894, and enter the churchyard by the small gate to the right of the lychgate. Walk round to the right of the tower past the impressive cedar trees to reach Laleham Road, turn left and pass the church's chestnut trees. Turn right into Gresham Road, and just beyond Budebury Road on the right take a signposted footpath to Spelthorne Leisure Centre and Civic Offices.

(This is a convenient place to join the walk from the station.) Follow the indicated footpath which becomes a pleasant leafy path, eventually passing a leisure centre, with an external water slide visible. The path becomes a road, passing various civic and public buildings, to arrive at a roundabout. Turn left onto the main road, cross it, and take a path opposite going round the side of the striking BAT offices. This leads to Priory Green; cross it and turn right to cross the brook – look out for

The old town hall, built in 1880.

ducks in the wild area to the left. Fine willow trees line the road.

Continue straight on past the end of two roads and the road becomes a track with a line of trees on the left, eventually veering left as it comes to the first part of Shortwood Common, open grassland with clumps of trees, and a fenced-off wood to the left. The track leads to a kissing-gate; go through this and with great care, looking both ways, cross the busy railway line. Go through the kissing-gate on the other side, turn right and go under the road bridge, entering the next part of Shortwood Common by the kissing-gate. Go diagonally across this following a grassy path, crossing a tarmac path to come to the pond at the other side. Turn left at the pond and follow its bank towards the road. The reed beds of the pond are home to swans and other waterfowl. At the end of the pond, turn left and follow the edge of the field to the corner, leaving the common by the kissing-gate opposite the Crooked Billet.

Cross Staines bypass on your left by the footbridge, then walk a little way down London Road (the next exit from the roundabout), crossing to the right. Pass the bus station on the left, then turn right onto Fairfield Avenue by the British Gas HQ. Turn right into Moormede Crescent, then right onto Waters Drive. Pass the end of Swallow Close on the left and turn right onto a path running beside a line of chestnut trees. At the end of the estate, the path veers left to pass between the backs of houses and a fence, then comes to the river Colne.

Shortwood Common.

Walk alongside the river up to the Staines bypass bridge. Go up the steps to the right, turn right at the top, cross the bridge and follow the footpath down along the road embankment. At a crossroads of footpaths, turn right to go under the bridge. Enter Staines Moor through a kissing-gate. Walk across to the half-left, towards the second pylon to the left of the river, then deflect slightly to the right on a moderately well-defined path, aiming for the gates in the fence. Go through the kissing-gate and under the abandoned railway line, turn left and cross the footbridge over the stream. Turn left at the public footpath sign and go through a kissing-gate to cross another railway line extremely carefully. At the other side, turn half-left and walk across the common to reach the pub.

Laleham
The Three Horseshoes

This is Laleham's oldest inn, possibly dating from the 15th century. Part of it was certainly an inn in the 17th century, and a 1768 tenancy agreement is framed on the wall. In extensions over the centuries the original front door of the coaching inn was blanked off, forming the 'horse box', a small front room where the Prince of Wales (later Edward VII) waited to meet Lillie Langtry. A reputation for assignations persists – numerous nooks and crannies certainly afford privacy.

Lovers of good food are also well served and a full range, from snacks, home-made soups and daily special main courses such as poached salmon, chops, quiche and grilled chicken, to excellent home-made desserts (served with real cream), can be ordered at the bar and eaten at tables anywhere in the bars, the new conservatory (where children are welcome) or the garden. There is a separate restaurant offering linen, waitress service and one or two additional menu items, but wherever you eat the food is prepared with care and imagination and portions are generous. Meals are served 12 noon to 2.30 pm and 7 pm to 9 pm (lunches only on Sunday).

The beers kept are Webster's, Ruddles County and Best Bitters, and Fuller's London Pride. The opening times are: Monday to Saturday 11 am

to 11 pm; and Sunday 12 noon to 4 pm, 7 pm to 10.30 pm (sometimes all day in summer).
Telephone: 01784 452617.

How to get there: The pub is at 25 Shepperton Road, on the right-hand side coming from Shepperton, before the church. Nearest station: Staines (BR), then walk along the river to join the walk at Pentonhook Lock.

Parking: While walking, please use the car park at the riverside or park elsewhere in the village.

Length of the walk: 2½ miles. Map: OS Pathfinder 1190 (inn GR 052688).

Laleham is a picturesque village in a conservation zone, with over 20 listed buildings and intriguing connections with some historical personages, from Edward VII to the Earls of Lucan. On the walk you visit the parish church of All Saints, then Penton Hook Island in the Thames, a haven for wildlife. Then after a pleasant rural riverside ramble you return to the pub via well-wooded Laleham Park, and Abbey Drive where several fine 19th-century houses survive.

The Walk

Leave the pub, turn right and walk along Shepperton Road. Pass Dial House on the right, named for the sundial replacing an upper window. Now enter All Saints' churchyard.

Pillars in the nave of the church and part of the west wall are 12th-century, the remainder being a mixture from many periods. There is an old tunnel connecting the church and the pub, continuing on towards the Abbey. The splendid stained glass window, depicting St Christopher, St Eustace and St Cecilia, commemorates an organist. The church is open to visitors 11 am to 5 pm in summer (school holidays; not Sundays).

Laleham is known locally as the Village of Widows; apparently a disproportionate number of women outlive their husbands. You can see some evidence of this on headstones in the churchyard. The Bingham family vault (east of the church) is where the 3rd, 4th and 5th Earls of Lucan are buried – the family home was Laleham House (now called Laleham Abbey). The 3rd Lord Lucan ordered the charge of the Light Brigade. The 7th Lord Lucan, missing since 1974, is still lord of the manor. One of his responsibilities is to appoint the vicar, so the inauguration of a new vicar is delayed for one year in case Lord Lucan turns up to raise an objection. So far, he hasn't.

Thomas Arnold, the celebrated headmaster of Rugby, began his career in Laleham. Matthew Arnold (1822–1888), his eldest son and a noted poet and literary critic, was born in Laleham and is buried here, near the

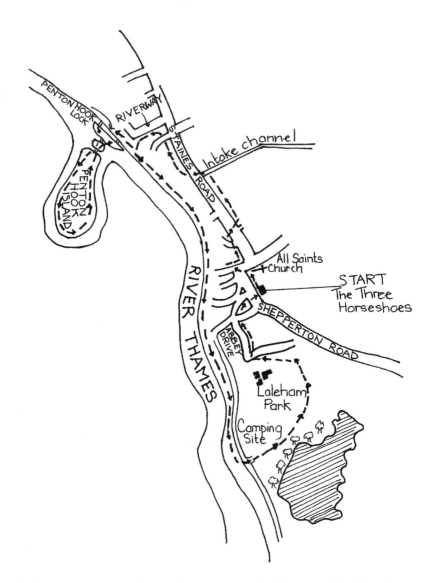

lychgate. He was professor of poetry at Oxford, memorably describing it as the city of dreaming spires and the home of lost causes.

Leave the churchyard, turn right and cross over busy Shepperton Road carefully. Cross Blacksmith's Lane, passing the war memorial. At the end of the lane is Plane Tree House, once the stables and laundry of the mansion house. The house next door down the lane was the forge (hence

Blacksmith's Lane). Veer right to continue along Shepperton Road past High Elms and Yew Corner, which were once, as one property, the Regency mansion house. Turn left onto Staines Road. At Cedar Close, by the magnificent cedar tree, cross over to use the pavement on the right, then back again after the water intake. Turn left into Riverway. Walk along here and turn left onto the public footpath to the riverside. Turn right to reach Pentonhook Lock and Island, opposite the lock-keeper's cottage (1814), by a row of chestnut trees.

The Thames makes an acute loop here. Penton Hook Island was formed between the original meander and the neck of the loop. The first lock was constructed in the neck in 1815. Cross over the lock-gate bridge and main weir to the island, which is a valuable wildlife habitat with a rich variety of flora and fauna – established since the 1940s, when dredging spoil was spread over the island. The salmon ladder opened at the weir in 1995 completes a chain of leaps from Teddington to Whitechurch.

Take the right-hand path to walk anti-clockwise around the island's river bank, passing a picnic area on the south-west side and a wetland area on the east. Look out for thrushes, finches and warblers in the trees and shrubbery, and herons and great crested grebe in the river and wetland area.

Leave the island and turn right to retrace your steps along the river bank. Pass the end of Blacksmith's Lane, opposite Harris Boatbuilders.

The river near Laleham Abbey.

The ferry ran from the end of Ferry Lane to the Surrey side until 1972. When Thomas Arnold became headmaster of Rugby, he moved his goods and chattels from Laleham to Rugby by barge, via the Thames and the Grand Union Canal. At the tarmac road, veer right onto the Thames path over grassland dotted with several large willow trees. Locals come here to feed the numerous Canada geese, swans and mallards which congregate on the grass.

Continue by the river as the grassland narrows. Pass Laleham Park camping site and a car park on the left, then cross the road and walk between the car park and a children's play area. Continue ahead across the open grassland of Laleham Park, fringed by broadleaf trees. Glimpse a water-filled gravel pit through trees to the right, and Laleham House to the left. The house was built for the 2nd Lord Lucan, who bought Laleham Manor in 1803. The 5th Earl sold the mansion to nuns and it became Laleham Abbey, a community of St Peter the Apostle. The nuns sold it to a property developer and it is now luxury flats.

Pass the clump of chestnut and rowan trees in the middle of the grassland, and a huge solitary plane tree nearby. Veer slightly right to take a path through a gap in the trees to the right of the wooden fence around the mansion grounds. The mound ahead on the other side of the drive covers the remains of the ice house. At the end of the Abbey fence veer left towards Abbey Drive and its parking bays. At the public toilet turn right to walk along the drive. The thatched cottage was the lodge to Laleham House. Pass The Coverts, a fine early 18th-century redbrick house, then at the junction with Ferry Lane turn right, passing Muncaster House, where Thomas Arnold and his brother-in-law opened a preparatory school at the beginning of the 19th century. Return to the pub along the lane.

17 Whitton
The Duke of Cambridge

This is a very pleasantly situated Watney Combe Reid pub, with more of a rural than urban atmosphere. The front, which has won at least one award for its appearance, has a shady patio with tables and chairs looking right across to stately Kneller Hall, and there is a very big garden at the back with children's play equipment (special prices are charged for children's soft drinks to attract families). Inside there is a friendly village pub atmosphere, a bar area with settles and stools, and probably the pub dog Dixon, a golden retriever.

On summer Fridays there is a barbecue 12.30 pm to 2.30 pm and 8.15 pm to 10 pm, with chops, kebabs, steak and sausages with appropriate accompaniments. There is also a standard lunch menu (available Monday to Saturday) of honest-to-goodness pub grub, all lovingly home-cooked, including various chip-based meals, steak with vegetables and potatoes and ploughman's lunches; bar snacks, but not meals, are available on Sunday.

Beers served are Webster's Yorkshire Bitter and Wadworth 6X, and the drinking hours are: Monday to Saturday 11 am to 11 pm; and Sunday 12 noon to 10.30 pm.

Check a Twickenham fixture list if you're planning a Saturday walk in the rugby season; the pub and surrounding streets get crowded on match days.
Telephone: 0181 898 5393.

How to get there: The pub is opposite Kneller Hall on Kneller Road (B361), linking Chertsey Road (A316) to Hanworth Road (A314). Nearest stations: Whitton, Hounslow and Twickenham (BR); Hounslow East (Piccadilly) and then bus 281 (from the bus station) or H22 (from London Road).

Parking: In the pub car park (but avoid match days at Twickenham).

Length of the walk: 4¾ miles. Map: OS Pathfinder 1174 (inn GR 147742).

After a stroll through the quieter streets of Whitton, the walk takes you through Crane Park, stretching along the river Crane and much of it left as wild habitat, including an island nature reserve on a former gunpowder factory plot. The walk follows the river through more formally laid-out parkland, and then a watercourse almost to the home of Rugby Union, returning to the pub in front of Kneller Hall.

The Walk

Leave the pub and turn left along Kneller Road. Pass the ends of Whitton Dene and Nelson Road, and then the old White Hart Inn on the left. Whitton in times gone by was a small hamlet west of Twickenham and this part has old inns and the sites of stately homes. You shortly pass Murray Park, once part of the grounds of Whitton Park, home of the architect William Chambers. The house was demolished about 1847.

Turn left at Vicarage Road, passing the church of St Philip and St James and its fine trees. Cross Hounslow Road and continue into the unmade Keswick Road. Bear left, continue down St Vincent Road, then turn right onto Nelson Road, almost opposite the library. Pass the Roman Catholic church on the left, then turn left into Hospital Bridge Road, crossing the railway line via the footbridge on the left. On the right there are now open fields behind the nurseries.

Enter Twickenham cemetery (open until 6.30 pm) by the first gate on the left, walk towards the far side and bear right. On the right amongst the headstones is a memorial to a number of variety artistes (their benevolent fund runs a local retirement home) including one, on the back wall, to Hylda Baker, who died in 1986 aged 81. Walk towards the chapels and continue towards the right-hand corner – on the right are First World War military graves of two Belgian soldiers, with their national flag on the headstones.

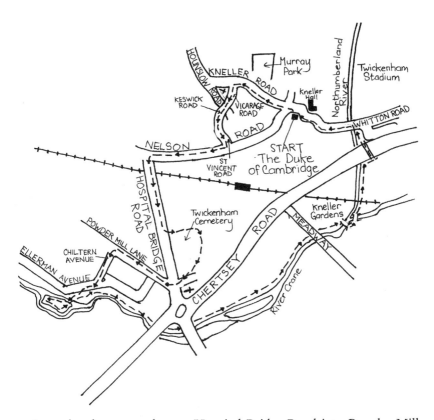

Leave by the gate and cross Hospital Bridge Road into Powder Mill Lane. Turn left at Chiltern Avenue, right into Ellerman Avenue, and then turn left at the footpath into Crane Park. Turn right at the tarmac path and continue to the brick tower, called locally the Shot Tower.

The river once fed watermills used in the gunpowder mills built on the adjacent island in the 18th century, and closed in 1926. The tower was probably not used for making shot, but would have been a water and firewatch tower – the mills suffered 55 explosions altogether. Cross the footbridge onto the island, which is now a local nature reserve. Once on the island, turn right to follow a path by the main stream. The centre of the island was once flooded to form a millpond and now contains a number of grasses and coppiced willows. Coming up to the end of the island, there is a concrete dipping platform, a favourite spot for children to study shallow water wildlife.

Now return via the obvious path following the backstream. You may see a heron, and possibly the edible frog. You pass mounds covering ruins of the powder mills and, following the path to the left to cut through the

Kneller Hall.

island, more mill ruins and a mixed broadleaf wood on the right.

Cross back over the bridge by the tower, turn right and follow the line of the river. This part of Crane Park also provides plenty of wild habitat in the form of grassland, trees and bushes as a 'green corridor'. Go under Chertsey Road Bridge and then Hospital Road Bridge. On the left is the distinctive shape of the redbrick church of St Augustine of Canterbury. You may see a water vole on the opposite river bank. Continue straight on, following a sign to Kneller Gardens, reached by crossing Meadway.

Take the path by the river, to the right of the tennis courts. Turn right at the white concrete footbridge, then left following a signpost for the River Crane Walk. Pass to the left of the Day Centre, then turn left at the signpost for the River Crane Walk route via the Northumberland River. The path runs between two fences until it reaches the Northumberland River, an artificial watercourse. Up ahead you can see Twickenham Stadium.

Follow the riverside path – although this is an artificial river the banks are overgrown and this also acts as a wildlife corridor. On your right is the Harlequins' rugby ground (The Stoop). Turn right at Chertsey Road, crossing it by the footbridge. Coming down from the bridge, go straight on for a few yards, then turn right, back onto the riverside path. Leave the river at the next road (Kneller Road/Whitton Road) and cross it. You are right by the English headquarters of Rugby Union. Internationals have

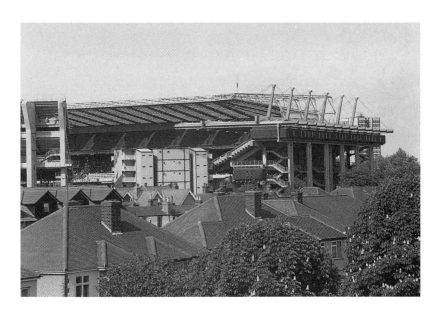

The headquarters of English Rugby Union since 1910.

been played here since 1910, but the present proud stadium is obviously a little newer. There is a new museum inside (closed Monday), and tours of the grounds may be arranged on non-match days – call 0181 892 8161.

Turn left along Kneller Road, passing the grounds of Kneller Hall. It was built for Sir Godfrey Kneller, painter of royal portraits, in 1709–1711, with 19th-century additions. The serious fence indicates its use as the home of the Royal Military School of Music. Open-air concerts are held on summer Wednesday evenings (call 0181 898 5533 for details). Continue along Kneller Road to return to the pub.

Hampton
18 The White Hart

The White Hart, facing the Triangle at Hampton, dates back to 1730, and as 'The Six Bells' was once owned by the 18th-century actor David Garrick. Oliver Twist and Bill Sikes called at a Hampton inn before a burglary at Chertsey – this may be the one Dickens had in mind. Nowadays, it is a freehouse sought out for its range of cask ales and so very much a pub for drinkers, who enjoy a choice pint in one of the nooks with comfortable upholstered benches and tables. There's even a rack of newspapers provided.

Hearty home-made pub lunches are served until 3 pm, Monday to Saturday; the portions are generous, the meals are well presented, and even familiar pub dishes are lifted out of the rut by being well herbed and seasoned and served with home-made chips. Filled jacket potatoes, salads and sandwiches are alternatives to the daily specials. A few ice cream based desserts are available. Some of the substantial filled rolls also offered at lunchtime may be available in the evenings. Children are not permitted in the bars, but there is a fair-sized patio at the front, with tables, chairs and umbrellas.

Eight handpumps are kept on the go, with Flowers, Abbot and Boddingtons ales as fixtures, and the others changing frequently for

variety. Drinking hours are: Monday to Thursday 11 am to 3 pm, and 5.30 pm to 11 pm; Friday to Sunday all day.
Telephone: 0181 979 5352.

How to get there: The pub is on High Street, Hampton, at the Triangle, off the A308 Hampton Court Road/Thames Street which runs by the river. Nearest station: Hampton (BR). Buses 726 (to Heathrow or Dartford) and R68 (to Hampton Court station or Richmond) pass the pub.

Parking: There is very little by the pub, so try the surrounding streets such as Ormond Avenue.

Length of the walk: 2¾ miles. Map: OS Pathfinder 1190 (inn GR 142697).

Starting with the small-scale 18th-century centre of Hampton village, the walk takes you past some grand 19th-century industrial architecture, then David Garrick's villa. You conclude with a stroll through a wooded portion of Bushy Park.

The Walk
Leave the pub, turn left into Church Street and walk down on the right. On the left are some fine 18th-century buildings. Orme House, No 4, is late 17th century and Old Grange is early 17th century. Opposite, No 9 was built around the turn of the 19th century, reputedly on the site of the home of Sibell Penn, nurse to Edward VI. Walk down the pathway to St Mary's church, rebuilt in 1831; there has been a church on the site since 1342. Circle it on the north side to pass the curious pyramidal tomb erected by John Grey's 'relict' Catharine, who herself died '. . . in the 82nd year of her age, full of years and benevolence'. On the south side lies the captain of Victoria's Royal Yacht; some burials appear to be those of former residents of Hampton Court grace and favour apartments. The monarch holds the manor of Hampton, as marked by the crown on top of the church flagpole.
Leave the churchyard by the gate facing the river. Turn right onto Thames Street, then right again into High Street and immediately left into Station Road. This has some good-looking 18th-century cottages and a fine redbrick 1905 police station. Pass the filter beds on the left, then turn left into Oldfield Road. Follow it round then turn left into Rose Hill, following the sign to the library, a noteworthy Georgian building bearing a couple of blue plaques, one to William Ewart (1798–1869) who promoted public libraries. Walk round the right-hand side of the library to see the landscaped garden and front of the building, then continue down the path to the road. Don't cross over, but turn left and concentrate on the industrial architecture in front of you.

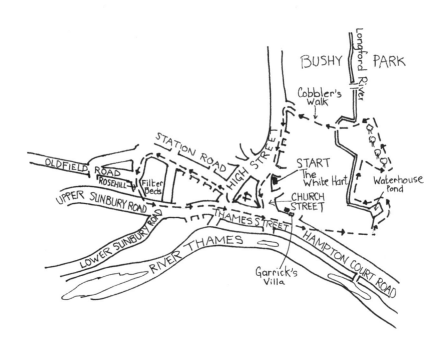

Victorian water companies frequently produced grand buildings and a sequence of them follows. The first, built for the Grand Junction Company, has two engine houses connected by a low boiler house. On the corner with Lower Sunbury Road is the Southwark & Vauxhall Company's engine house. Past the end of the road is the same company's huge Morelands building – two engine houses connected by a 14-bay boiler house. Last and grandest, the Riverdale building, with a boiler house resembling a parish church connected to an engine house built like an E-plan stately home. The original gatehouse and clocktower, no longer on the Thames Water site, have recently been refurbished by a private developer.

As you continue along Thames Street, passing the end of High Street and in front of the church, you walk over a giant water main far below, which goes from the water works all the way to Chingford. Pass the end of Church Street to continue along Hampton Court Road. On the left is Garrick's Villa, once the home of the celebrated actor (probably Hereford's most famous son) and opposite, by the river, is the temple he had built to house Roubiliac's sculpture of Shakespeare.

Continuing, you come to 'Garrick's House' (which does not seem to have been) on the right, and almost hidden behind wall and railings on the left is the White Lodge, built as the focal point of Lime Avenue in Bushy

Garrick's villa.

Park. Enter the park through Hampton Gate on the left, turn right and walk down the centre of Lime Avenue until you reach the tarmac path on the left to the gate into the Woodland Gardens. (No dogs are allowed in the gardens. If there are canines present, follow the perimeter fence round to River Lodge Gate and rejoin the walk there.)

Follow the path by the stream on the left through the gardens, which were laid out in the 1940s. At the Waterhouse Pond follow the bank of the pond round, passing the Canadian Pergola and then, on your right, the Canadian Glade with its totem pole. The pond is fed by Lord Longford's River at the north-west end. Take a path following the river course from this end of the pond – the start may be a little overgrown, a few feet away from the bank at first, then the path follows this artificial river. At a 90° bend to the right in the river you get a good view over the fields of Hampton and its church. Marshy areas in the fields opposite attract birds, and you may see a heron. At intervals you pass take-offs feeding the streams in the gardens. When the river turns sharp left, leave it and head back down the hornbeam avenue at 135°, then leave the gardens at River Lodge Gate.

Turn left and continue through Bushy Park following the fence on your left, then at a tarmac path turn left to go through a gateway. This is Cobbler's Walk, a right of way since 1752. Continue between fences – on the right is a wildlife conservation zone. Cross the Longford river by the

Deer in Bushy Park.

footbridge. After passing the swimming pool on the right (a public one, in case you're feeling hot), turn left onto High Street. A number of houses along this road are noteworthy, especially 18th-century Grove House (No 100), No 90 (Hampton House) with a bay above the door supported by columns, and No 78, with white gables either side of a redbrick centre, topped by a cupola, visible after you pass. Returning to the pub, you have a good view of the 18th-century terrace facing the Triangle.

Hammersmith
The Dove

This is a marvellously atmospheric, historic pub, owned by Fuller's since 1796 but an inn for much longer, having reputedly served Charles II and Nell Gwyn. Its many literary and theatrical patrons include A. P. Herbert, who lived locally, and James Thomson, who wrote the words to *Rule Britannia* here. Immediately to the right of the front door is what must be the smallest bar in London. Through the main ground floor bar and up a staircase is a comfortable room and food servery. Beyond that is a conservatory and a terrace overlooking the river.

Excellent lunches are served every day, 11 am to 3 pm, including four or five substantial daily specials, such as haddock in pasta or beef in ale, served with a choice of jacket, sauté or croquette potatoes and tasty fresh-cooked vegetables. There is a large range of salads, quiches, pasties and ploughman's lunches, or jacket potatoes with various fillings. On Sunday to Thursday evening, from 6 pm to 10 pm, this traditional English pub fare metamorphoses into Thai cuisine. No hot food is served on Friday and Saturday evening, but rolls may be available. Despite the warning above the front door, children may eat inside with their parents and dogs on leads are tolerated, but not in the busy evening time.

Fuller's ESB and Fuller's London Pride are on handpump, and drinking hours are Monday to Saturday 11 am to 11 pm, and the new all-day Sunday hours.

Telephone: 0181 748 5405.

How to get there: The pub is at 19 Upper Mall, Hammersmith, W6, off Furnival Gardens. Access by car is from the A4, heading west. Take the first left from the Hammersmith Flyover, then left again. Nearest stations: Ravenscourt Park and Hammersmith.

Parking: No pub car park! Parking is very restricted near the pub. Come by public transport, or use the car park at Chiswick House (on the walk), or the NCP multi-storey King's Mall car park near Hammersmith station on Glenthorne Road (closed Sundays, when parking meters are free).

Length of the walk: 4 miles. Map: OS Pathfinder 1175 (inn GR 226783).

From Hammersmith, you walk along a fine part of the riverside to reach Chiswick church, pay homage at the tombs of two artists and marvel at the architecture of Chiswick House, before returning to Hammersmith by way of Turnham Green and Ravenscourt Park. The gardens of many of the grand riverside houses are open on a Sunday in May under the National Gardens Scheme.

The Walk

Leave the pub and turn left into Upper Mall. At No 26, Sir Francis Reynolds constructed the first electric telegraph in 1816. William Morris also lived here, weaving Arts & Crafts fabrics on a loom in the bedroom, giving Socialist lectures in the coachhouse, and running the Kelmscott Press. The basement is now home to the William Morris Society. Continue by the river, passing Weltje Road and a blue plaque for the artist Eric Ravilious. After the sailing club, go under the archway and pass the sea-green pub, the Old Ship.

After Upper Mall Open Space, turn right and then left to follow Hammersmith Terrace – grand houses with colonnaded porches and Roman numerals, and riverside rear gardens. The author A. P. Herbert lived and died at No 12. Continue along Chiswick Mall. On the left, behind the separated gardens of the mansions on the right, the river reappears; Chiswick Eyot is a wild habitat for birds. Pass Morton House and Strawberry House (both dating from 1730), then Walpole House, the home of Barbara Villiers (Charles II's mistress before Nell Gwyn). Just before this 'royal' house is a rare 'republican' pillar box (lacking a royal monogram).

At the end of Chiswick Mall is the parish church of St Nicholas. This is

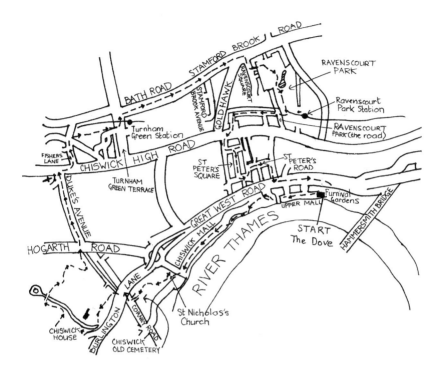

mainly 19th century, but the tower dates from the 15th century. A church has been here since 1181. Walk through the churchyard, between the church and William Hogarth's tomb, surrounded by railings and topped by an urn. Turn right at the railing, then turn left to walk past the closed churchyard. Enter Chiswick Old Cemetery through the gateway, continuing along inside on the path following the wall, to reach Whistler's conspicuous bronze tomb against the wall.

Continue straight on, and turn left at the first tarmac path. Follow this past the end of the wall on the right then turn right to pass a large memorial to Frederick Hitch (1856–1913), who gained a VC at the battle of Rorke's Drift in 1879 – a soldier portrayed in the film *Zulu*. Leave the cemetery by the gateway onto Corney Road and turn right. Cross Burlington Lane (use the nearby pelican crossing) and enter the grounds of Chiswick House (grounds open until dusk) by the gate opposite Corney Road. Turn left, then turn right to approach the front of the house.

Visit the house, if you wish (opening hours: summer, daily until 6 pm, winter, Wednesday to Sunday until 4 pm; admission fee, or free to English Heritage members). The Palladian-style villa was designed by Lord

Chiswick House.

Burlington himself to display works of art and entertain visitors; this it still does. It is one of London's most pleasing buildings.

Return to the front driveway and, facing the house, turn left and walk to the cascade at the end of the lake. Like much of the landscaping, this is by William Kent. Continue by the wall, to the obelisk. Take the avenue heading 20° towards the Ionic Temple visible across the lake, then at the lake turn left and follow it to the bridge. Cross over and take the central of three paths, then the first tarmac path left. Shortly after turn right onto a well-defined rough track, heading off at about 75°. Turn right at a T-junction onto a tarmac path and enter the central avenue of a *patte d'oie* (a group of paths radiating out in the shape of a goosefoot) near the 'Venetian window' feature. Turn right onto the avenue, then left into a break in the hedge to reach the 'bowling green' (now not very flat), surrounded by broad-girthed sweet chestnuts. Leave the green by its right-hand edge and bear right to reach a break in the hedge of the next avenue from the *patte d'oie*, crossing straight over to follow a path by the wall. Before you reach a tall column, go left through the gateway and follow the path to the car park and Hogarth Road exit.

Cross the busy A4 by the subway into Duke's Avenue. Continue to the end, by a 1904 redbrick Roman Catholic church, with a 1930 tower by Gilbert Scott added as a war memorial. Cross Chiswick High Street, turn right, then left into Fishers Lane. Go onto the Common, turn half-right into the avenue. At the end, cross Turnham Green Terrace. Turn left, go under the railway then turn right onto Bath Road. This is the focus of Bedford Park, a Victorian garden city development; St Michael's church (left) and the Tabard Inn (right), inventive, delightful buildings by Norman Shaw, were built 1879–80.

Continue past Priory Gardens estate, and turn right after Prebend Gardens into Stamford Brook *Avenue*, then immediately left into an unnamed side street to pass No 27, The Brook, where the artist Lucien Pissarro (Camille Pissarro's son) lived. Return to Stamford Brook *Road*, and continue past St Mary's, a church built in 1886 and converted into flats in 1986. Go straight on where Goldhawk Road merges from the right, then turn right into Ravenscourt Square and left into Ravenscourt Park.

Palingswick Manor and grounds were acquired for this public park in 1887. It contains many interesting trees and an avenue leads to the site of the house, destroyed in 1941. Walk across to the pond, a magnet for waterfowl, then turn right to follow it. At the end, head over to the right to follow the edge of the park south. The large red-brick building is the 1931 Royal Masonic Hospital. Skirt a play area, go under the viaduct into a smaller section of the park and pass the sundial to exit on the right into Ravenscourt Park (the road), then turn left into Hamlet Gardens. Walk through the central garden in Westcroft Square and turn left.

Cross King Street and enter St Peter's Square, a little to the right. At the square proper, turn left and then right to walk down the left side of this fine Georgian area, then turn left at the end to approach St Peter's, built in 1829 and Hammersmith's oldest church. Turn left into Black Lion Lane, right into St Peter's Road, then right into the cobbled Beavor Lane/Albert Terrace.

Turn left at the Great West Road, and cross it by the subway near the Town Hall. Take the left subway exit to enter Furnival Gardens. There is a good view of Hammersmith Bridge from here. Turn right into the alleyway to return to the pub.

Strand-on-the-Green
The Bull's Head

There may have been a pub here for 350 years. There is a story that Oliver Cromwell was drinking here when visiting his sister, who lived in Chiswick, when he was betrayed to the Royalists and fled via a tunnel to the neighbouring island in the Thames. Nowadays it's a very popular pub with a mixed clientele, royalist and republican, and an atmospheric sprawling interior, plenty of separate rooms, some overlooking the river.

Food is available every day from the downstairs servery until 10 pm (Sunday meals 12 noon to 4 pm), although more choice is available at lunchtime than later on. Hot daily specials include home-made steak and kidney pie, chicken Kiev, chilli con carne and usually a couple of vegetarian choices, all served with seasonal vegetables or salad, as well as main course salads and generous ploughman's lunches. Hot and cold desserts, served with real cream, are available and the soft ice cream machine is popular in summer.

Drinking hours are: Monday to Saturday 11 am to 11 pm, and Sunday 12 noon to 10.30 pm, and the beers served are Theakston Bitter, XB and Best, and one or two guest beers.

Telephone: 0181 994 1204.

How to get there: The pub is on Strand-on-the-Green, Chiswick, next to the railway bridge, with car access at the rear on Thames Road – turn left onto Strand-on-the-Green just before Kew Bridge heading south. Nearest stations: Gunnersbury (District line and BR North London line); Kew Bridge (BR).

Parking: There is a small pub car park. Car parking is available at the north end of Gunnersbury Park, and the steam museum has a car park for visitors.

Length of the walk: 4 miles. Map: OS Pathfinder 1174 (inn GR 197776).

The walk starts along an attractive section of Thames riverfront and proceeds to Kew Bridge Road and two unusual museums: the Kew Bridge Steam Museum and the Musical Museum. You continue to Gunnersbury Park, with sweeping lawns, flower beds, avenues of many species of mature trees and the Gunnersbury Park Museum.

The Walk

Leave the pub, turn right and walk past Oliver's Ait (or Island) on the left, named after Cromwell's supposed escape; a tunnel from the pub to there would have to be long and deep. Pass some fine old riverfront houses, noting particularly the blue and white shuttered Dutch House, and the blue plaque to the German painter Johann Zoffany (1734–1810), portraitist to George III. At the end of the path continue along the Strand-on-the-Green.

At Kew Bridge turn right and cross Chiswick High Road on the left to reach the Express Tavern. Turn left and walk along Kew Bridge Road towards the Victorian chimney stack. To visit Kew Bridge Steam Museum, turn right onto Green Dragon Lane. Otherwise continue ahead. The museum, open daily 11 am to 5 pm, is housed in a 19th-century pumping station. The main exhibits are five Cornish beam engines, including the world's largest working example. Some may be seen in steam at weekends. Admission fee. (0181 568 4757).

From the museum return to Kew Bridge Road. Turn right and walk to the Musical Museum (0181 560 8108) which houses a large collection of automata, from musical boxes and nickelodeons to the country's only player Wurlitzer. Allow 90 minutes for an enthusiastic guided tour, 2 pm to 5 pm, April to October Saturday and Sunday only, except July and August, Wednesday to Sunday. Admission fee.

From the museum turn right and right again onto North Road. Turn left at the North Star then right onto Clayponds Lane. Cross over Green Dragon Lane and the railway bridge, continue ahead and turn right to enter Carville Hall Park. Walk through the park, passing Carville Hall on

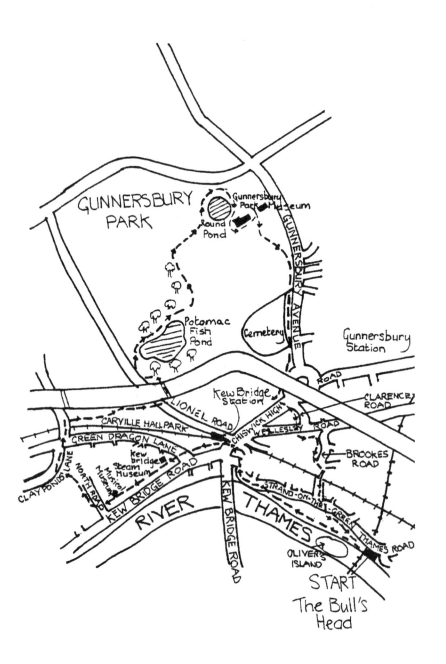

GUNNERSBURY PARK

Round Pond

Gunnersbury Park Museum

Potomac Fish Pond

Cemetery

Gunnersbury Station

GUNNERSBURY AVENUE

ROAD

CLARENCE ROAD

Kew Bridge Station

LIONEL ROAD

CHISWICK HIGH

WESLEY ROAD

BROOKES ROAD

CARVILLE HALL PARK

GREEN DRAGON LANE

Kew bridge Steam Museum

Musical Museum

CLAYPONDS LANE

NORTH ROAD

KEW BRIDGE ROAD

RIVER

STRAND-ON-THE-GREEN

KEW BRIDGE ROAD

THAMES

OLIVER'S ISLAND

THAMES ROAD

START
The Bull's Head

94

the right. Leave the park at the far side and turn right, cross over Lio Road and cross the A4 via the subway. Turn right from the exit into Lio Road and enter Gunnersbury Park at Gate 7.

Gunnersbury Park Estate dates from at least the 13th century. An earl owner was Edward III's mistress, Alice Perrers. It was later the summo. residence of Princess Amelia, daughter of George II. The last single owner was the Rothschild family. It has therefore been landscaped by the finest artists and planted with a variety of fine trees. At the fork veer left and turn immediately left onto the path skirting the Potomac Fish Pond, veering round to the right. At the end of the pond continue ahead, and turn left at the T-junction. After passing a children's play area (and toilets) on the right, turn right. Continue ahead and fork left at the Round Pond, created by the landscape artist William Kent in the 18th century. The Temple, by Sir William Chambers, halfway around the pond, is the only remaining building from the time of Princess Amelia, who often held dinners there; the Rothschilds used it as a synagogue.

Continue around the pond, pass a café on the left, then take the first left and follow the path to the 18th-century Western Arch. The Large Mansion was built in 1802, then improved in 1835 when the estate was bought by Nathan Mayer Rothschild who had established the British branch of Rothschild's Bank. After 1917 the estate no longer had a single owner, and in 1925 the Large Mansion and 126 acres of land were purchased for public use by two London Boroughs and Middlesex County Council to save it from being turned into an airfield. The park was opened in 1926 by Neville Chamberlain.

From the arch walk across the front terrace, turn left and left again to the entrance of Gunnersbury Park Museum. It has a well-displayed, eclectic collection, including a local history section. The interior includes an outstanding Victorian staircase and the lovely painting *The Four Seasons* by Edmund Thomas Parris (1793–1873) on the Long Gallery ceiling. The museum is open in summer 1 pm to 5 pm weekdays and 2 pm to 6 pm weekends, and in winter 1 pm to 4 pm weekdays, 2 pm to 4 pm weekends, admission free (0181 992 1612).

Leave the museum, retrace your steps to the front terrace and turn left to face the 19th-century Eastern Arch. The 19th-century Small Mansion beyond the arch is now the Mansion Arts Centre. Facing the Eastern Arch, take the path to the right. Pass the Orangery on the right, designed for Nathan Mayer Rothschild. Go straight ahead at the crossroads. To the left are the 'Gothic Ruins', a folly designed in the 1830s. Pass another folly, then veer left to follow the perimeter of the park, and leave by Gate 8. Turn right, walk along Gunnersbury Avenue and enter Gunnersbury Cemetery on the right.

Many members of Britain's Polish, White Russian, Ukrainian and Armenian communities are buried here, and in 1976 a memorial to the

.cre of 14,500 Polish prisoners of war was placed here.
.nclude those of Sir Carol Reed (1906–1976), director of
.; Sir Matthew Smith (1879–1959), the painter, who studied
.; General Bor-Komorowski, who ordered the Warsaw
.d Prince Vsevolod (1914–1973), great-great grandson of Czar
. and cousin of Nicholas II.

the cemetery, turn right and continue to the Chiswick
.bout. Turn right and go under the Chiswick flyover, via two
.n crossings, to the Esso petrol station. Turn left and cross Chiswick
.h Road by another pelican crossing. Turn right and then left onto
.arence Road. At the T-junction turn left onto Wellesley Road and then
.ight onto Brookes Road. At the end cross the footbridge over the railway
line and continue straight ahead. At the top turn left onto Thames Road to
return to the Bull's Head on the right.